Axiology:
The Science of Values

D1565351

VALUE INQUIRY BOOK SERIES

VIBS

Volume 2

Robert Ginsberg

Executive Editor

Axiology:
The Science of Values

Archie J. Bahm

Amsterdam - Atlanta, GA 1993

An earlier version of this book was published by the author for private circulation, copyright 1980 by Archie J. Bahm.

ISBN: 90-5183-519-1 (CIP)
©Editions Rodopi B.V., Amsterdam - Atlanta, GA 1993
Printed in The Netherlands

To

Kiren

Books by the Author

Ethics: The Science of Oughtness

Ethics as a Behavioral Science

What Makes Acts Right?

Why Be Moral?

Philosophy: An Introduction

Metaphysics: An Introduction

The World's Living Religions

Comparative Philosophy

The Philosopher's World Model

CONTENTS

Foreword

Archie J. Bahm has written a frank and mature defense of the science of values as a major field of knowledge that stands on its own power while also serving other valuable fields of knowledge ranging from economics to aesthetics. He makes room for the big shoulders of axiology among the crowd of respectable sciences in this scientific age. Bahm's case for the scientific status of axiology is presented from a comprehensive view of all knowledge, yet he gets into the detailed substance of the distinctions that flow from the field. Thus, he clarifies central subjects of Good and Bad, Ends and Means, Actuality and Potentiality, and Objectivity and Subjectivity as applied to values, while he explores our coming to know values and our terminology for them. This work is foundational yet relational, for it focuses on the social context of knowledge. People are at the heart of knowledge and value.

Bahm's vision is informed by cosmopolitan experience in several areas of human value, including religion, the arts, and moral activity, and he has a keen sense of the standards for scientific method. This succinct and pungent text will give second thoughts to those who regard science as above or beyond values as well as to those who regard values as merely emotive, exclusively personal, or otherwise unscientific. As he has done throughout his distinguished career, Bahm throws bridges across the notorious gap between the two cultures of the sciences and the humanities. He does so here with the vigor and freshness of informed inquiry. More than just an able introduction to value science, this book is a spirited defense of our humanity as knowers, judges, and beings of value.

Robert Ginsberg
Executive Editor

Preface

Values, good and bad, are omnipresent in human experience. Everyone understands values as enjoyed and suffered, yet the theories formulated about them have created doubts. How should you decide what values are?

Science is reputed to have the acceptable methods for achieving reliable knowledge these days. Yet science has adopted a partly false philosophy, Positivism, claiming that science is or ought to be, completely value-free. This philosophy relieves scientists from responsibility for investigating values and prevents them from doing so as scientists. When you desire to understand values, you must seek information elsewhere.

I was trained to believe that scientific methods ought to be used in solving philosophical problems. My philosophy of science is Pragmatic rather than Positivistic. My theory of values can be tested personally by scientists and by you and all other persons.

Archie J. Bahm

1

One

WHY AXIOLOGY?

The value of values is self-evident. This work is not so much about values as about axiology, the science of values. Values have existed as long as human beings, and longer, since animals also experience values. All of the pre-historical developments bringing human beings into existence functioned as instrumental values.

Trying to understand the nature and kinds of values has been a perpetual problem. Despite multitudes of theories, some of them persisting for millennia as guides for civilizations, the best word for characterizing the current situation is "confusing." I do not mean that no clear and definite solutions exist. In fact, some theories are proclaimed as dogmatic ideologies. But growing doubts about traditional doctrines and proliferation of new conjectures characterize current uncertainties. Personal speculations about the nature of values, nurtured not only by long-prevailing ideals of freedom of thought and speech but now also by spreading ideals of permissiveness (freedom without responsibility), contribute to present chaos.

Axiology is valuable in many ways. These will be summarized in two groups. The first is more general, the second more specific. The first pertains to the nature of axiology and its role in normal times, the second to the urgent need for it at present. The first evaluates it as a science among sciences, the second evaluates it as a vital tool for understanding critical personal, megalopolitan, national, and global problems. The two groups will be named (1) axiology as a science and (2) relevance to crisis solutions.

1. Axiology as a Science

A. Axiology is One of the Three Most General Philosophical Sciences.

The three inquire into existence ("metaphysics"), knowledge ("epistemology"), and values ("axiology"). All other sciences may be located in one of these three areas, although some specific sciences involve inquiries of all three areas.

The distinction between existence, knowledge, and value does not imply that what is distinguished is thereby separated. Knowledge and values exist, and as such are properly investigated by metaphysicians. Existence and values are known, and as such are properly investigated as objects of knowledge by epistemologists. Existence and knowledge have value, and as such are properly investigated by axiologists. But the distinctions between existence, knowledge, and values provide bases for distinguishable kinds of questions and of inquiries into these questions.

Axiology, as the science inquiring into values, is thus one of the three most general kinds of inquiry, and thereby is one of the three most important kinds of science.

Each kind of inquiry - each science - has its own primary contribution to make to human understanding. Each is superior to all others with respect to its contribution. Axiology inquires into goodness which is a condition of inquiries into existence and knowledge (and the inquiries constituting all other sciences). That is, we inquire because inquiry is good. Axiology, in inquiring into the goodness involved in inquiry, has the goodness of all other inquiries, that is, of all other sciences, as its particular contribution to all other sciences, including the general sciences of metaphysics and epistemology.

B. Axiology Is the Most Basic Value Science.

There are many value sciences. These include aesthetics: the science of beauty, ugliness and fine art; ethics: the science of oughtness, duty, rightness and wrongness; religiology; the science inquiring into the ultimate values of life as a whole; and economics: the science of wealth and illth relative to the production, distribution, and consumption of goods. Some sciences are more obviously value sciences because they deal directly with some values. The foregoing involve subsciences dealing with values: the psychological, sociological, and political sciences, as well as historical and anthropological studies, all involve values in their inquiries.

Since beauty and ugliness, rightness and wrongness, wisdom and folly, income and expenditures all involve goodness and badness, then understanding the general, specific, and particular problems in aesthetics, ethics, religiology, and economics, etc., involve understanding goodness and badness. Thus, axiology is significant because successful achievement in its inquiries is required for fully successful achievements in all other value sciences. they depend on it. In performing its function as the most basic value science, axiology is the most important value science.

C. Axiology is Needed by Non-Value Sciences.

Many sciences do not intend to make values objects of their inquiries. Axiology makes no direct contribution to understanding things that do not involve value. But sciences as inquiries involve problems, attitudes, methods, and successes and failures. Each science involves concern with such questions as to whether a problem is a genuine problem, is clearly conceived, and is likely to be solvable with appropriate efforts. Since scientists believe that inquiry will be better when their problems are genuine, clearly conceived, and likely to be solvable, their beliefs involve goodness.

Each scientist has the scientific attitude, which involves curiosity, open-mindedness, willingness to be guided by experience and reason, willingness to suspend judgment until sufficient data are available, and willingness to hold conclusions tentatively. Each of these is a good characteristic of the scientific attitude, and having the scientific attitude is better than not having it; in fact, having it, and its goodness, is essential to science. Each scientist uses some method, usually involving gathering data, formulating an hypothesis, and testing the hypotheses. Each wants good data, a good hypotheses, and good tests. Idealizing the goodness of data, hypotheses, and tests, that is, of methods, is inherent in science. Although scientific inquiries often involve many trials and errors, scientists naturally believe that it is better to make as few errors as possible, and that final success in solving a problem is a good to be sought and, when achieved, a good realized. In all of these ways, every science, including those that do not make values objects of their inquiries, inherently involves values.

If the value aspects of non-value sciences are to be understood scientifically (and what other way would a scientist want them to be understood?), then scientists in these sciences depend on axiology as a science for inquiring into the nature and kinds and ways of functioning inherent in all sciences In this way, axiology has an useful contribution to make to all sciences, including the non-value sciences.

The magnitude of these three values of axiology as a science is a measure of the deficiency of the scientific community in neglecting to include it as a recognized science.

2. Relevance to Crisis Solutions

Awareness of accelerating national and global crises urgently calling for solution spurs my efforts to pressure the scientific community to recognize and support axiology as a basic science. Its usefulness will be observed relative to causes of our crises, to understanding our crises, and to overcoming our crises.

A. Negligence of Axiology as a Cause of Our Crises.

Our crises, national and global, are of many kinds and result from many causes. Having surveyed some of these elsewhere,[1] I limit consideration here to causes involving values and, specifically, (a) to misunderstanding values and (b) neglect of axiology.

    i. *Misunderstanding of Values.* That our crises problems are essentially value problems should be clear to everyone. But that values are misunderstood is not so clear. There are many reasons for these misunderstandings. Values are complex in their natures, and yet they often appear simply as feelings. Such feelings are difficult to describe. Explanations that have developed, in folklore, ancient scriptures, early philosophies, sectarian schools, and in popular mores, have contributed to culturally inherited misunderstandings and confusions that few can escape. Theories developed by scientific specialists, such as psychologists, physiologists, anthropologists, sociologists, economists, and aestheticians, reflect influences of both specialized viewpoints and sectarian schools of thought.

    When persons responsible for policy decisions face actual decisions, the value theories called on, implicitly or explicitly, reflect prevailing confusion and biased explanations. When disagreements occur and appeal is made to the excuse, "There is no disputing about taste," efforts to seek truth about values are abandoned. When each person's opinion counts as equal to that of others, and decisions are based on votes, the result is determined by which biased opinion happens to be most prevalent among those voting. When no demonstrable basis for value decisions is available, decisions reflect quantitative bias. When this is the case, those who would succeed will seek converts to their biases. Special interest groups then rightly increase pressures in support of their views. Increase in group membership, often involving population increase, becomes the way to promote decisions favoring its bias. This kind of thinking is used to justify racism, nationalism, and loyalty to political, religious and any other kind of ideology. But conflicts arising from such movements are among the primary causes of current crises. So long as genuine understanding of the nature of values is missing, continuing acceleration of conflicts caused by such lack of understanding can be expected to increase.

ii. *Neglect of axiology.* The scientific community, which could challenge sectarian theories by recognizing axiology as a science, by developing its demonstrable principles, and by including these in its science education programs, could then demonstrate the falsity of mistaken views. But it has failed to do so. Many scientists too have been captured by sectarian philosophies of science, and some of these that exclude value from scientific consideration happen to have achieved predominance. There are historical reasons why such philosophies were adopted by scientists. Need for freedom from biasing influences when performing experiments aiming to be objective readied scientists for accepting a philosophy of science claiming to free them from such biases. But they mistakenly adopted another bias, a bias against value judgments which is itself a basic value judgment that has been questioned more often recently. By causing neglect of axiology, the scientific community has contributed to a condition in which policy deciders have not had reliable information that may have prevented some of our crises problems.

B. Importance of Axiology for Understanding Our Crises.

If we cannot overcome our crises until we understand them, and if we cannot understand them as value crises until we understand the nature of values, then recognizing and developing axiology, the science devoted to understanding the nature of values, is necessary for overcoming our crises.

Axiology alone, i.e., as a most general science, cannot provide sufficient understanding to overcome our crises because they are extremely complex, and understanding them will require information drawn from many of the sciences. Major problem solutions now require multiscientific contributions and more and more interscientific, or interdisciplinary, research. Understanding our crises will require understanding also the nature of oughtness, a major task of the science of ethics. But ethics, as a science of right choices (wise policy decisions) such as choosing the better of two or more alternatives, presupposes understanding the nature of good and bad, better and worse, or of values. Part of the significance of axiology is its providing a necessary foundation for ethics as a science. Intrinsic values are the ultimate bases for moral appeals. They are also the ultimate bases for economic, political, educational, and religious appeals. So axiology is needed for understanding our crises, partly because it is important for understanding the nature of ethics and other sciences that depend on ethics.

Contributions from still other sciences, such as psychology, sociology, economics and political science, are needed for understanding our crises. But these sciences too, as value sciences, depend on axiology. Scientists in these fields cannot understand the value aspects of their problems fully until they too achieve the kind of understanding sought through axiology. Thus, part of the importance of axiology is to be found in its services to other value sciences that provide information essential to understanding our crises.

C. Values of Axiology in Overcoming Our Crises.

As long as value conflicts constitute our crises and no method, short of war, can be agreed upon for resolving them, doomsday warnings seem warranted. If persons responsible for policy decisions can be persuaded that a science of values exists and that its demonstrated principles can be relied upon, then they should feel warranted in considering any demonstrations needed because they have found scientific demonstrations reliable in dealing with other problems. These demonstrations will have to be rigorous. If the demonstrations are convincing, deductions concerning decisions and behavior commitments should follow. When this occurs, the usefulness of axiology for overcoming our crises will be demonstrated.

Axiology as a necessary means for overcoming our value crises is of interest not merely to the scientific community, which should want the science established, developed, and used, but also to the whole community, to the nation, which has a stake in human survival, and to humanity. The urgency of our needs for crisis solutions implies urgency for the development of axiology. It should be given top priority by those concerned with national interest and human survival. A crash program is needed, both to make up for lost time and to bring results to bear quickly on our problems.

Two

WHAT IS SCIENCE?

Fully conceived, science involves six major kinds of components. These pertain to problems, attitude, method, activity, conclusions, and effects. Some minimal understanding of each component is essential for full understanding of the nature of science.

1. Problems

No problems, no science. Scientific knowledge results from solving scientific problems. No problems, no solutions, no scientific knowledge.

What makes a problem "scientific"? Are all problems scientific? No. If not, what then characterizes a problem as scientific?

Differing answers to this question by scientists and philosophers of science are so various that general agreement soon seems impossible. I propose, as an hypothesis, that a problem can be regarded as scientific only if it has at least the three following characteristics, pertaining to communicability, to the scientific attitude, and to the scientific method.

A. No Problem Is Properly Called "Scientific" Unless It Is Communicable.

I am sure that some will insist that, to be scientific, a problem must already have been communicated. But when competent scientists have discovered a problem and have worked on it privately for a long time before communicating their conclusion to others, it seems unreasonable to judge that their private work was not scientific in any sense. Communicability seems sufficient. But problems that are incommunicable do not achieve the status of "being scientific."

B. No Problem Is Properly Called "Scientific" Unless It Can Be Dealt With by Means of the Scientific Attitude.

See "attitude" below.

C. No Problem Is Properly Called "Scientific" Unless It Can Be Dealt With by Means of the Scientific Method.

"Wherever the scientific method cannot be applied, there cannot be science...." See "Method" below (Weisz, 1961, 4).

Being scientific is a matter of degree. Science exists in its fullest sense when all of the six components outlined here exist to their fullest capacity. But science exists, as problems, already in problems. Problems that are being dealt with by the scientific attitude and method are more scientific, or more fully scientific, than those problems that are dealt with without them. Problems that are well along toward solution are, in a sense, more scientific than those on which work has just begun. Problems that have been solved, so that their problematic character has diminished considerably, are, in a sense, still more fully scientific. Problems that interrelate other scientific problems and solutions systematically (and more adequately in providing greater understanding) are in a sense more fully scientific than problems that are treated in isolation from other problems and solutions. But, I propose, problems that are communicable and capable of being treated by means of the scientific attitude and method are already, in an initial sense, properly called "scientific."

2. Attitude

The scientific attitude includes at least six major characteristics: curiosity, speculativeness, willingness to be objective, open-mindedness, willingness to suspend judgment, and tentativity.

A. Curiosity.

But not idle curiosity. Scientific curiosity is concerned curiosity. It is concern about how things exist, what is their nature, how they function, and how they are related to other things. Scientific curiosity aims at understanding. It develops into and continues as concern for inquiry, investigation, examination, exploration, adventure, and experimentation.

Some scientists have scientific curiosity about some things but not about others. Some are trained to hold the scientific attitude toward problems within their specialized fields, without developing feelings of obligation to inquire into other problems and of acquiring, or carrying over, the scientific attitude relative to them. But some scientists tend to make the scientific attitude a part of their life outlook, so that they retain a tendency to be curious about all things.

B. Speculativeness.

But not idle speculation. To be scientific, we must be willing to try to solve our problems. We must make some effort. When, as is usual, the solution to a scientific problem is not immediately obvious, effort must be made to discover a solution. We must be willing to propose one or more hypotheses that may serve as solutions. We may have to explore several alternative hypotheses. We must be willing to risk unsubstantiated opinion in making initial proposals. Initial hypotheses often are highly speculative, and every new hypothesis, except perhaps those derived deductively from established principles, involves some speculation. Speculativeness is clearly intentional and necessary in developing and trying out working hypotheses. In these ways, speculativeness is an essential characteristic of the scientific attitude.

C. Willingness to be Objective.

"Objectivity" is one kind of subjective attitude. The willingness to be, and the effort to be, objective has come to be regarded as essential to being scientific because such an attitude is better, is more conducive to the achievement of reliable results. Those who mistakenly divide the polar opposites, "objectivity" and "subjectivity," into contradictories completely excluding each other, may be admired for the intensity of their desire for reliable results but must be condemned as ignorant of, or at least as ignoring, their essential interdependence. Objects are always objects for subjects; no subject, no objects; no subjectivity, no objectivity. Objectivity depends for its existence upon the willingness of the subject to acquire and hold an objective attitude, that is, an interest in understanding the nature of objects themselves, insofar as they can be understood in this way.[1]

I propose that the willingness to be objective includes:

i. *Willingness to follow scientific curiosity wherever it may lead.* I do not mean that we must be willing to endanger our lives or livelihood or those of others, but that we should be willing to be curious and concerned about furthering inquiry needed for understanding as much as prudently possible.

ii. *Willingness to be guided by experience and reason.* Extreme empiricists and rationalists often try to separate reason and experience. Extreme empiricists assert that sensory experience is the only source of knowledge. Extreme rationalists assert that only beliefs that conform to rational laws can be true. Such extremists often disagree about the nature and reality of universals and particulars. Extreme empiricists hold that we can have certain knowledge only of particulars, that is, of particular sensory experiences in which data are intuited. Extreme rationalists hold that we can have certain knowledge only of universals, and of valid deductions from them; somehow the universal forms must be intuited as well as the deducible implications. But actually universals and particulars interdepend and interact in experience (Bahm, 1974b, 78-94), and processes of scientific investigation depend on success in interrelating them. Although tentativity is also required for the scientific attitude, enough trust in generalizations based on past experience and in deductions based on demonstrations of logical validity is needed to enable a scientist to proceed with investigations on the basis of them. Demonstration that an hypothesis involves a contradiction is sufficient reason for rejecting it.

Before leaving reason, we should observe two meanings of reason that are sometimes distinguished and even separated. On the one hand, reason is conceived as conformity to rational law.[2] On the other hand, reason is conceived as ability to choose the better, or best, between two or more alternatives. That is, when choosing between two alternatives one of which appears to be better than the other, what is the reasonable thing to do? Choose the better. Actually these two meanings interdepend, for those who advocate being reasonable as conformity to rational law do so because they believe such conformity to be better. In choosing the better of two alternatives, one is already conforming to a rational law. The willingness to be guided by experience and reason includes the willingness to be reasonable in both of these ways.

iii. *Willingness to be receptive.* Data, something given in experience when objects are observed, are received as evidence relevant to a problem being solved. The scientific attitude includes a willingness to receive data as they are, uninterpreted by biasing preferences of the observer. Receptivity involves a willingness to take what is given for what it is, or appears to be, without willful, or even willing, distortion. Granted that each observing mind brings with it some preconceptions and a somewhat fertile imagination and that these often participate unintentionally in scientific observations. The willingness to be objective involves a willingness to achieve understanding by maximizing reception of what is received from objects and by minimizing subjective factors (that is, preconceptions, imagination, preferences).

Granted that data uninterpreted by biasing preferences are useless until related to an interpretive hypothesis, and that many scientific data are sought deliberately to confirm (or refute) an hypothesis and that such deliberate seeking often embodies biasing preferences. Nevertheless faith that the hypothesis itself, if it succeeds in solving the problem, will reflect the real structure of the problem so that it serves as an instrument for achieving truth about the object itself, can embody willingness to be objective.

Although each formulation of an explanatory hypothesis involves both some discovery (observation of facts about the object or problem) and some invention (ideas intending imaginatively to construct a conception of the object or problem), the willingness to be objective involves a preference for discovery and a willingness to forego invention as much as possible. Objectivity means that the object, not the subject, is the authority, the source of the knowledge sought by the scientist. So long as the authority refuses to reveal its nature, the scientist must speculatively invent. But willingness to be objective involves readiness to receive more data regarding the object or problem being investigated, because understanding, which is the aim of scientific investigation, is achieved to the extent that something about the nature of the object is revealed from the object. Although the Aristotelian interpretation of knowledge as "in-form-ation," somehow getting the form of the thing to be also the same form in the mind, is much too simple for contemporary scientists, it embodies an ideal of objectivity, namely, that the primary source of understanding of objects is in the objects.

iv. *Willingness to be changed by the object.* Whenever a scientist discovers something that he did not know before, the scientist becomes changed by the addition of this new knowledge. Such changes may seem insignificant to a scientist who has desired to acquire some knowledge and then has the previously-existing desire satisfied. But some scientific discoveries result in scientific revolutions, that is, in radically changed conceptions of the nature of things, including selves, societies, atoms, and galaxies. These require the scientist, as willing to be objective, to revise and reconstruct his conceptions of himself as well as of other things. If one is unwilling to become changed in any way required by the results of successful scientific investigation, then he lacks something of the willingness to be objective.[3]

Current clamor about global crises resulting from rapid technological changes has popularized evidence of how much people's lives have been changed as a result of scientific developments. Scientists need not go so far as to join a Federation of Atomic Scientists and feel compelled to regret publicly the consequences of their discoveries. Nevertheless a willingness to be aware of the possibilities and prospects of changes resulting from their investigations and a willingness to be influenced by such changes and to become changed all seem to be implied in the willingness to be objective.

v. *Willingness to err.* Trial and error methods are so characteristic of science, and the quantity of the errors occurring before each success is so great, that a scientist must expect to spend much more time in efforts resulting in errors than in achieving the truth. To the extent that each error, each erroneous hypothesis eliminated, is instrumental in bringing investigations to final success, each must be regarded as having instrumental value and thus as worthwhile in its own way. A person who demands success on a first trial lacks something essential to the scientific attitude.

Although "objectivity" pertains primarily to the objects being investigated, it also pertains to the methods used in trying to understand the objects. For objects are such that they yield information when some methods are used but not when other methods are used. Thus, the willingness to be objective uses the methods required by the objects. The willingness to be objective involves willingness to err whenever an inadequate method is used and willingness to overcome the error by another, better method. The willingness to be objective may involve a willingness to be frustrated as often as is needed during the processes of investigation.

This willingness to err should not detract from the unwillingness to err, also characterizing the scientific attitude. But this characteristic, that is, the intention to be truthful, both to accept the truth and to tell the truth, is such a fundamental and obvious presupposition of the scientific enterprise that it does not call for mention. In a sense, the willingness to be objective and the willingness to be truthful are identical. It may be that, if current progressive demoralizing trends continue and infect scientists as they have other sectors of our society, the necessity of willingness to be truthful as a characteristic of the scientific attitude may become less obvious to many; if so, then it should receive emphatic mention.

vi. *Willingness to persist*. Although no rules exist for how long a scientist must persist in grappling with an intractable problem, the willingness to be objective implies willingness to continue trying to understand the object or problem until understanding has been achieved. A person who willingly gives up trying when frustrated in many efforts to understand gives up something essential to the scientific attitude. We may have to stop because our budget gives out. But this need not cause us to give up our willingness to try further.

D. Open-mindedness.

The scientific attitude involves willingness to be open-minded. It includes willingness to consider all relevant suggestions regarding hypotheses, methodology, and evidence relative to the problems on which the scientist is working. It tolerates, and even invites, new ideas, including those differing from, and those appearing as contradictory to, the scientist's conclusions. As long as evidence remains inconclusive, open-mindedness includes willingness to hear and examine the views of others and unwillingness to condemn without sufficient reason.

F. Willingness to Suspend Judgment.

When the investigation of an object or problem does not yield desired understanding or solution, then, as scientific, a person is willing not to demand more answer than is available. The scientific attitude suspends judgment until all necessary evidence becomes available. This implies willingness to remain uncertain, and to retain whatever patience is required by such continuing suspension.

G. Tentativity.

Not only should unproved hypotheses, including working hypotheses, be held with an attitude of tentativity, but the whole scientific enterprise, including each specialty, remains somewhat dubious. Although personal and group experiences warrant firmer convictions regarding conclusions as they continue to work longer and better and more fully (through harmonious inter-relation with conclusions held in other fields), proof of certainty always remains less than one hundred percent (the percentage available from deductive proof).

Studies in the history of science provide evidence that scientific systems that become established and almost universally accepted in one era have always remained inadequate and have given way eventually to revolutionary conceptions that led to the establishment of new systems based on radically different pre-suppositions (Khun, 1962). Historical evidence, at least, indicates that the firmest convictions now held and the most intricate and most adequate interpretive systems prevalent may yet give way to something more adequate. As long as this possibility remains in prospect, dogmatism regarding currently accepted conclusions is unwarranted. The scientific attitude remains tentative regarding all scientific conclusions. This implies a need for remaining undogmatic about methods, since different conclusions may depend for their establishment on differing methods needed to establish them.

The foregoing interpretation of the scientific attitude portrays the scientist as forever experiencing a tension between tenacity and tentativity. On the one hand, persistence is needed for holding on to an hypotheses as long as it is the best available. On the other hand, since the best conclusions are never fully warranted, the scientist must remain unsure. Even though the suffering may not be great, a scientist must be willing to suffer whatever tensions are required by embodying the double willingness to be tenacious and to remain tentative.

3. Method

My proposals regarding the scientific method must be regarded as hypotheses for further testing. The subject is extremely controversial.

On the one hand: "What makes a study scientific is not the nature of the things with which it is concerned, but the *method* by which it deals with these things" (Thompson, 1911, 38). "The essence of science is its method" (McGrath, 1950, 118). "Science [as theories] is something that is always changing. The theories of today are not those of a hundred years ago.... Is there something...about science which does not change...? I think there is, and it is the method" (Ritchie, 1923, 14). On the other hand: "With regard to the nature of scientific method scientists themselves are not always possessed of clear and sound ideas" (Cohen, 1949, 48). "In any case, there is no unanimity about methodology among scientists themselves" (Jevons, 1893, 51). "The scientific method, like the Abominable Snowman, has been the object of an enthusiastic but on the whole unsuccessful search. ...The search has yielded up a number of somewhat bewildered scientists;...leaving the searchers no more enlightened than before" (Caws, 1965, 276).

A. Method Versus Methods.

The controversy and confusion results, I suggest, partly from neglect to relate the problem to distinctions between science and the sciences. Even here, controversy persists. On the one hand: A reason for interpreting "...the scientific method as though there were one and only one method is that the similarities between different applications of it in different sciences are greater than the differences. ...Full abstraction discloses that there is only one scientific method" (Fiebleman, 1971, 7). On the other hand: "Not science but sciences. ...There is no single science, but only a series of families of sciences" (Kantor, 1953, 5).

My response to this controversy about whether scientific method is one or many is that there is some truth to both views. Scientific method is both one and many.

i. *It is one.* "There is no subject matter to which scientific method cannot be applied" (Ross, 1971, 95). The nature of this method will be examined more fully below.

ii. *It is many.* In fact, it is many in many ways:

(1) Each science has its methods best suited to its problems. Obviously biologists must use microscopes, while astronomers must use telescopes; and biologists use control groups while astronomers cannot control their objects. "Each particular science will vary considerably in its methods..." (Ross, 1971, 95). The methods of different sciences

are so distinctive that some persons are tempted to classify sciences on the bases of differing methods. But differences in problems are what originate and differentiate the sciences. Different sciences develop different methodologies because different problems require different methods.

(2) Each particular problem may require its own unique method. "It is the problem which determines the method. ...there will be as many different scientific methods as there are fundamentally different problems" (Northrop, 1947, 19). "There are no rules to follow; each experiment is a case unto itself." Even within one science, many different methods develop. Gordon Alport found that psychology of personality alone employed about fifty-two particular methods (Alport, 1937, xiv). The quantitativeness of differing methods is evidenced by the *Guide to Scientific Instruments, 1973-74,* containing more than 25,000 individual entries (*Science*, 1973, 9-178).

(3) Historically, scientists in the same field in different areas used methods differing considerably because of differences both in theoretical development and technological invention. Even though previous methods have become obsolete, must we not recognize their scientific character because of their contributions to earlier scientific achievements?

When a major pervasive scientific revolution is occurring (Kuhn, 1962), different methods receive differing emphases as the new systematizing proceeds. Earlier stages are more inductive, that is, more working with particular methods in particular sciences. At later stages, not only more intermingling of methods but also more concern with synthetic problems and synthetic methods occurs. Still later, as the system becomes established and generally accepted, then deductive methods become more common, for consistency with the system becomes a primary requirement.

(4) Today, rapid development of many sciences and technologies, which more and more interdepend, requires rapid development of new methodologies to deal with more intricate and dynamic kinds of problems (such as electronic computers). Not only do sciences borrow methodological ideas and techniques from each other whenever appropriate, but the emergence of multidisciplinary approaches to complex problems calls for the development of new interdisciplinary methodologies.

(5) Even those who concern themselves with "the scientific

method" must recognize that this method itself has several stages which require different methods at each stage. "A scientific method is relative to the stage of inquiry with which one is concerned as well as to the type of problem" (Northrup, 1947, 38).

B. The Scientific Method.

I propose that "the scientific method" includes five steps or stages. This proposal is made against the background of a predominantly British Empiricist tradition in philosophy of science, which is usually interpreted as distinguishing four major steps: observation of data, classification of data, formulation of hypotheses, and verification of hypotheses. Issues regarding "data," including "sense data," as abstractions already partly interpreted, or misinterpreted, raise questions about whether observation of data is the starting point of scientific inquiry.

American Pragmatism has made some fundamental contributions to philosophy of science that are overlooked by many scientists as well as by many philosophers of science. The British Empiricist claims that hypotheses are verified by tracing them back to original sense data. But this is impossible. The sense data of one moment are gone the next, so the scientist must depend on memory or notations or records at best. The American Pragmatist claims that hypotheses are verified by their workability, that is, by how successfully they guide the practitioner to a future solution. If the solution predicted by the hypothesis achieves desired results, then it was, and is, true. But verification depends on data (desired results) observed *after* the hypotheses is formed. The Empiricist claims that persons look backward to previous data; the Pragmatist claims that persons look forward to future data. The difference is fundamental.

The two philosophies presuppose different conceptions of knowledge. Extreme empiricists depict persons born with blank minds waiting to be filled with sense data, which are then shaped by images and combined and recombined by actions of the mind. Pragmatists assume the biological principles of struggle for existence and survival of the fit, and interpret mind, ideas, and science as instruments evolved to aid in such struggle. When a person whose life is endangered gets an idea that aids in survival, both the person and the idea survive. If the idea fails, both the person and the idea perish. Less serious problems, such as how to grow food, build and contain fire, or domesticate animals, likewise require ideas. Those that help solve these problems survive and are used again. Those that fail are discarded and perish.

The two philosophies differ thus somewhat regarding the originating step in the scientific method. Empiricists: "All science begins with *observation*, the first step of the scientific method. ...After an observation has been made, the second step of the scientific method is to define a *problem*. In other words, one asks a question about the observation" (Weisz, 1961, 4,5). Pragmatists: "The task of the first stage of inquiry is the analysis of the problem." The task of the second stage "is to inspect the relevant facts designated by the analysis in the first stage. ...the method of observation, the method of description, and the method of classification" (Northrop, 1947, 34,35).

Although some may regard differing about whether the scientific method begins with an observation or a problem as quibbling, since a person does not become aware of a problem without observing, and an observation does not become scientific until it arouses interest (becomes problematic), nevertheless these differings beget differences in conceptions of how to proceed. Those who begin by observing data proceed naturally to analysis of data, such as sense data. Those who begin by being disturbed by a problem proceed naturally to an analysis of the problem. The problem itself determines what data are relevant and functions as a guide to observations as well as to the kind of hypothesis needed for its solution. I favor the view that science is a problem-solving enterprise and thus see the scientific method as having the characteristics essential to problem-solving methods.

In proposing five steps as essential to the scientific method, I am stating a theory not only about them but also an ideal about how these steps should be taken. I am aware that, in practice, scientists do not follow this pattern step by step but commonly jump back and forth from one to another many times. Often a scientist has to formulate an hypothesis and begin testing it before it is possible to decide reliably which data are genuinely relevant to the initial problem. Furthermore, as accepted scientific conclusions become more complicated, many problems originate as technical difficulties such as systemic inconsistencies or experimental limitations, so that it now seems possible that a person employed as a scientist may never have an opportunity to experience the challenge of an original problem initiating a series of stages of the scientific method. "It certainly is not the case that conscious attention to explicitly formulated methodological principles is necessary for success in practice" (Jevons. 1893, 51). I do propose, though, that when any one of the five characteristic stages is missing from a scientific investigation, something essential is missing from the full application of the scientific method.

Although I am indebted to many others (Dewey, 1938), my sketch of the five steps is my own and does not fit precisely that of any other thinker. But I propose it here as a basis for further discussions with those who refuse to recognize axiology as a science because they hold differing, more restricted, conceptions of science. The five stages: i. Awareness of a problem. ii. Examining the problem. iii. Proposing solutions. v. Testing proposals. vi. Solving the problem.

i. *Awareness of a problem*. No problem, no science. Awareness of a difficulty in understanding provokes doubt about beliefs.[4] The difficulty may be long-standing or newly discovered. If a person feels helpless, hopeless, or incompetent to deal with the difficulty, it does not become a scientific problem. A person can, and relative to some problems must, accept incompetence. A person must have a desire to deal with the problem and to try to solve it before it can qualify as scientific.

ii. *Examining the problem*. Examination of a problem begins by observing it. This is initiated by an interest in the problem and by an effort to understand it. Although interest in understanding the problem may be continuous with interest in understanding its solution, initial efforts are focused on understanding the problem. These are efforts to clarify the problem, that is, both to mark out its boundaries and to analyze its ingredients. Such clarification aims to distinguish relevant from irrelevant aspects of the problem. It provides bases for distinguishing relevant from irrelevant data (and consequently relevant and irrelevant hypotheses).

Initial examination of the problem is likely to include an effort to evaluate the importance of the problem, that is, whether or not, and how much, effort should be exerted to solve the problem. This evaluation will involve others: Is the problem solvable? Is it solvable within the limits of time, money, effort, and cooperation required? What are the probabilities that it can and will be solved? What values can be expected from achieving a solution?

Examining the problem is likely to generate questions about causes of the problem, how it is related to, or interrelated with, other factors in experience, and whether and how it is like similar problems dealt with previously. These questions involve inferences about such causes, other factors, and other problems. Problem solvers often remark that "Well begun is half done." The more fully a problem is understood, the more likely a workable solution will be achieved. Thus, thoroughness and carefulness in examining a problem are prescribed as beneficial in scientific method. The more highly socialized a scientific inquiry, the more attention needs to be paid to expressing clarifications in language easily and clearly communicable to other scientists. Accuracy as well as adequacy in observing, analyzing, and communicating a problem are excellent ideals for a good beginning.

iii. *Proposing solutions.* Solutions, to be adequate, must be clearly relevant to the problem. Initial suggestions often spring spontaneously from initial observations of the problem. But progressive clarification of the problem usually refutes initial suggestions yet leads to others seemingly more adequate. Trial and error thinking is to be expected. Some problems, when clearly understood, generate solutions almost immediately. Other problems resist clarification and obvious solution. When a problem defies efforts to propose relevant solutions, scientists often try out "working hypotheses," hypotheses relevant to only some of the main features of the problem. Then by exploring implications of such hypotheses, they may discover additional data relevant to further clarification of the problem or refutation of the working hypothesis.

iv. *Testing proposals.* Two kinds of testing ("verification of hypotheses") can be distinguished: mental and operational.

(1) Any hypothesis suggested, early or late in an investigation, should be examined mentally before other efforts are expended on it. Criteria for a good hypothesis have been suggested: (a) Consistency, within itself, with known facts, and with the prevailing body of scientific theory. (b) Relevancy of the hypothesis to the problem and evidence available. (c) Adequacy in comprehending all relevant factors, in revealing theoretical understanding, and in providing for testability and final solution. (d) Clarity and simplicity are desirable, but clarity should include what is clearly unclear, while simplicity that reduces adequacy falsifies. (e) Communicability, especially easy communicability, when possible.

Although reasoning occurs at every step in the scientific process, it receives special emphasis during mental testing because mental tests are primarily rational in nature. Consulting with colleagues during mental testing is especially beneficial, because deficiencies in the hypothesis, including any failure to embody the criteria of a good hypothesis, can be detected and corrected more easily before efforts are invested in costly operations. As science becomes more complicated, criteria for numbers and kinds of colleagues to be consulted are established; at the same time, the more highly specialized a scientific investigation becomes, fewer colleagues are available for consultation. Growing awareness of the increasing importance of interdisciplinology should have the effect of encouraging, if not requiring, inquiry into and evaluation of implications of the hypothesis for other fields.

(2) Operational testing, often involving designing one or more experiments, aims to demonstrate the workability of the hypothesis. It involves observation of new evidence tending to verify or refute the hypothesis. Each science, often each problem, will require its own kind of experiments and its own instruments for measuring. Each kind of experiment will have its own criteria for excellence. In addition, operational testing is better (other things being equal) when it is more efficient (yields more evidence, verifying or refuting the hypothesis for less costs in time, money, equipment, and effort), when it provides more conclusive evidence, and when it is more easily repeatable, as well as when it better continues to embody the criteria cited for mental testing.

The ideal experiment is called "crucial" because it is designed to determine definitely and finally whether an hypothesis is true or false. Crucial experiments are difficult to design, especially as problems become more complex and include more factors. Increasingly evidence is stated in terms of probabilities, including, where possible, estimations of probable error. So hypotheses are "verified" only approximately, or in some degree, and, in many cases, only under limiting conditions.

v. *Solving the problem*. Problems may remain scientific even when they are not solved. Problems may remain scientific even when they appear to be unsolvable by presently known methods. But the aim and purpose of scientific method is to solve problems. Problems originating in doubt are not fully solved until that doubt has subsided and investigators feel satisfied that understanding has been achieved.

The initial problem, plus additional problems arising during the investigation, determine the criteria for satisfactory solution.

If a doubt arises in a single mind, that mind will have its criteria for settling its doubts. If problems do not become scientific until they become social, that is, have been communicated to at least one other scientist, then solutions do not become scientific until they become social. Problems of publications, distribution, reading, and understanding solutions are involved in the way that scientific problems are finally solved. Does full solution require translation into all languages? As scientific periodicals proliferate with increasing numbers of specialties, and as specialists complain that they cannot keep up with even specialized publications, do solved problems, including those accepted by some as fully demonstrated, suffer from deficient solution in the sense of reduced attention by other scientists?

Presuppositions

"There is no presuppositionless research" (Bunge, 1967, 181). Although each of the six components involves presuppositions, recognition of presuppositions is especially relevant to method. For difference in presupposition can make a difference in how problems are conceived, in what constitutes a relevant hypothesis, in what kinds of tests are required (or permissible) for verification, and in how reliable conclusions can become.

Minimal presuppositions include assumptions about existence and its knowability (metaphysical), about mind and its capacities for knowing (psychological), about knowledge and how it is obtained, retained, modified and forgotten (epistemological), about language and communication (linguistical), about the structures of thinking and inferences and their relations to things thought about (logical), about numbers, calculations and mathematical inferences (mathematical), and about values, such as beauty, obligations, and the ultimate values of living (axiological, aesthetic, ethical, and religious). These presuppositions are subjects of inquiry by the philosophical sciences.

But scientific method also presupposes assumptions about the physical universe (occurring as conclusions, and assumptions, of the physical sciences), about life (occurring as conclusions, and assumptions, of the biological sciences), and about society (occurring as conclusions, and assumptions, of the social sciences). The task of seeing how all of the parts of the existing universe function together in some kind of whole belongs to philosophy performing its comprehensive function. Scientific method is involved in presuppositions about such comprehensiveness. The point is that the reliable conclusions of all other sciences can and should function as presuppositions, implicit when not explicit, of each science.

Not all scientists are aware of all of these presuppositions. Perhaps no scientist has succeeded in being aware of all of them relative to any one investigation. Some persons do function as if they were completely unaware of presuppositions. Yet they do not escape presupposing because they presuppose that they can function without presuppositions. Often presuppositions explained during a learning period function unobtrusively as mental background. Most scientists and philosophers of science too often attend to only a few of them. A philosophy of science is not fully adequate until it recognizes that the demonstrated conclusions of all sciences function as essential presuppositions of each science, at least to the extent that all contribute to any attempt to achieve a full understanding of existence, as a whole and in all of its parts.

One of the reasons for growing interest in interdisciplinary research is that information about conclusions in other sciences which must be presupposed has come to seem increasingly relevant, and significant, for solving problems in particular fields. In turn, increasing concern for understanding presuppositions results in greater awareness of the results of interdisciplinary research (Bahm, 1980).

Complicating the task of understanding presuppositions of science is the fact that many different schools of thought have developed which often have biasing effects on scientists' views about their presuppositions. Some schools arise relative to only a particular problem which may not have significant implications for other problems or other sciences. Other schools explicitly assert universal principles that do have implications for all sciences. Some of these schools are of ancient origin, and claim privilege for doctrines asserted in revealed scriptures (for example, God created the world according to an eternal plan). Some of these arise as political ideologies (Marxist dialectical materialism). Some result from efforts to achieve a more adequate physics (general relativity). Some result from rationalizations of mathematical certainties as having ultimate ontological status (Logical Realism). Others result from fear of rational tyranny and a quest for intuitive certainty in sensory particulars (British Empiricism).

I do not see how we can avoid the biasing effects of such schools of thought at the present time. But to the extent that their biases have a detrimental effect on the methods and results of scientific investigations, awareness of them and wariness about them is needed if we are to improve the quality of our scientific achievements. Those desiring to improve science as the way to better understanding and more effective problem solving should urge the development of another science, presuppositionology, for the purpose of achieving more objective treatment and more reliable conclusions about the presuppositions naturally inherent in the nature of science.

4. Activity

Science is what scientists do. What scientists do is often called "scientific research." Such research has two aspects: individual and social.

A. Individual.

"Science is an activity, a mode of practice...by particular men" (Ross, 1971, 1). In this sense, science exists in persons and nowhere else. It depends for its continued existence upon transference from person to person. "Only if we understand the scientist himself, examine his observations and see him actually observing, forming hypotheses, testing them by controlled experiment, and having those flashes of insight which are genius or akin to it, can we truly understand science" (Rapport, 1963, 43).

If you are a scientist, you are a product of your training, your opportunities for developing scientific interests, skills, and abilities, and usually opportunities for employment that further simulate and direct your more advanced development. Your activities become more or less those of a specialist (Bahm, 1977c). Your activities become molded by the tasks you have to perform, the instruments and processes with which you deal, the measurements and calculations that you must make, the laboratory or other environment in which you work, your colleagues and their habits, standards, knowledge, opinions, and morale. As a scientist, you are a person whose scientific activities interdepend with your other activities, those contributing to your health and well being, those in your roles as spouse, parent, citizen, etc., and those influenced by your phobias, manias, tolerances, and hopes. Scientific activities require adaptability, sometimes to routine and sometimes to novel problems. These require ability to withstand the tensions for dealing with frustrating problems, frustrating tools, frustrating colleagues, and frustrating employers, and with people in personal, family, and political life that often interfere with each other. Scientists sometimes become unemployed, ill, drafted, and sometimes must seek employment, and move, readjust, and retrain.

Scientists also prepare reports of their investigations, articles, and books or publications, and sometimes participate in conferences and conventions of scientific societies, local, state, regional, national, and international, more often those relevant to their specialties but at times to more general meetings of the American Association for the Advancement of Science. Some communicate with many other scientists while some work primarily in isolation. Scientific activity includes communication, or lack of it, between scientists within each specialty and between specialties. Learning, speaking, and writing specialized languages facilitates specialized communication yet inhibits interspecialty communication. Activities of many scientists have become departmentalized in ways that prevent interdepartmental communication. The activities of those trying to overcome the evils of departmentalization are also properly called scientific.

B. Social.

But scientific activity includes much more than what particular scientists do. "Science...has become a vast institutional undertaking" (Feibleman, 1971, 2). "Scientists are the most important occupational group in the world today" (Snow, 1962, 127). "Science, then, turns out to be an enormous accumulation of specific jobs" (Kantor, 1953, 2). Growth in scientific activity may be suggested by the increasing number of persons listed in *American Men and Women of Science*, 4,000 in 1903 and 290,000 in 1960.

Scientific institutions, including universities, research institutes, government bureaus, and corporation divisions in which scientific research occurs, require financing. Thus, the activities in private and public systems financing scientific research, especially those assuring

continuation of scientific efforts, must be included. Growth and
decline in funding affect scientific activities and thus must be regarded
as significant conditions of the existence and nature of science. The
quantity, quality, and kinds of scientific activities may be affected by
favorable and unfavorable attitudes toward science by the general
population, politicians, and business executives having influence on
funding policies.

Scientific activities include those involved in the processes of giving
up previously held theories and adopting new theories. Most scientific
activity presupposes that the scientific community has an agreed-upon
philosophy of science and a body of sound conclusions.   When
conflicting ideas arise, the scientific community "often suppresses
fundamental novelties because they are necessarily subversive of its
basic commitments" (Kuhn, 1962, 5). But when changes proceed to
the point that may become a crisis, scientists become disturbed.
Increasing evidence of the necessity for a new philosophy and revised
conclusions creates tension. "Creative scientists must occasionally be
able to live in a world out of joint" (Kuhn, 1962, 79). The temptation
and tendency of conservatives with vested interests to become
dogmatic in their expressions and the felt necessity by radicals to insist
on openness to demonstration and revision produces antipathies,
antagonisms, and sometimes persecution also characterizes scientific
activity.

5. Conclusions

"Science is knowledge obtained..." (Taylor, 1949, 17). "Science is
often conceived as a body of knowledge" (Singer, 1959, 1). "This
body of ideas is itself science..." (Mees, 1946, 48).

Conclusions, that is, the understanding achieved as a result of
solving problems, are the goals of science. They are the ends which
justify its attitude, methods, and activities as means. They are the
fruits of labor and investment. They are science accomplished, not
science as prospect or in process. They are what the scientific
enterprise is all about. Their importance is what justifies popular
impressions that science consists of reliable knowledge, or, better, in
certain knowledge.

However, most scientists recognize that scientific conclusions
remain   uncertain.   Not   only   do   some   distinguish   between

"hypotheses," "theories," and "laws" as representing increasing degrees of acceptance, but all should keep in mind that the tentativity essential to the scientific attitude requires that conclusions be held undogmatically. "The demand for scientific objectivity makes it inevitable that every scientific statement must remain *tentative forever*" (Popper, 1959, 280). No matter how useful and reliable a conclusion has been in theory and in resulting practice, when held with a dogmatic attitude, it lacks something essential to the nature of science.

A glance at the history of science reveals that "The science of one age has often become the nonsense of the next" (Singer, 1959, 1). "The science of today will look as foolish in a century's time as that of a century ago does now.... There is nothing in the world as ephemeral as a scientific theory" (Ritchie, 1923, 14). "Nothing in science is finally known" (Ross, 1971, 19). "Science is essentially or inherently unstable." (Agassi, 1975, 1) "Every succeeding generation is sovereign in reinterpreting the tradition of science" (Polanyi, 1946, 16).

Those who seek or claim certainty for scientific conclusions resent evidence for uncertainty. But professional scientists rationalize frustration by pointing out that progress in science has come not only by discovering new hypotheses but also by discovering that older theories are false. Some see science as a process in which each conclusion is a stepping stone for the next advance. "Every conclusion is fallible, but it must still be used as a premise for further investigation" (Ross, 1971, 19). "Popper's view is that a theory is scientific if and only if it can be overthrown with the help of experience" (Agassi, 1975, 25).

Despite continuing uncertainty and expectation that understanding everything is unrealistic, nevertheless the idea of progressing to greater approximation of understanding existence continues as a part of the scientific spirit. In spite of the increasing diversity of scientific interests and activities, exemplified by a growing number of specializations, subspecializations and sub-subspecializations, leading to the claim that there are only sciences (or subsciences) and no science, an ideal that all additional knowledge somehow supports all other knowledge, so that humanity is making some headway in mastering understanding the world, exists as a part of science. The task of understanding how all of the scientific conclusions as parts fit together in a comprehensive whole remains, and efforts toward achievement of this task receive another shock with each new major scientific revolution. The task is neglected in an age idealizing analysis, increasing specialization, and individual freedom of opinion and expression. The more complex scientific conclusions become, the more difficult does the synthetic task become. But to eliminate the ideal that science is making progress in achieving greater understanding of existence is to deprive it of something surely essential to it.

6. Effects

Science is what science does. Part of what it does is to produce effects. These effects are multifarious. Consideration of them here is limited to two kinds: 1. effects of science on technology and industry, through what is called applied science, 2. effects of science on, or in, society and civilization.

A. Applied science.

"What is sometimes termed 'applied science' may be more truly science than what is called pure science.... Thus conceived, knowledge exists in engineering, medicine and the social arts more adequately than it does in mathematics and physics" (Dewey, 1925, 161).

In what ways may applied science be "more truly" science?

i. *The very words, "applied science," connote extending science through its embodiment in applications.*

ii. *Although the immediate purpose of science is increased understanding, the purpose of science includes the larger purpose of improving conditions of living.* Some scientists explicitly state that the goal of their endeavors is to improve human welfare. To the extent that this is so, the nature of science includes this larger purpose.

iii. *The effects of science, beneficial and harmful, often become more obvious to people in its applications.* People achieve more appreciation of the values of science, and even some incentives to understand and support science better, when benefitting from its applications.

iv. *Financial support for further scientific inquiry comes more likely when governments and corporations experience its beneficial results.* "There is no getting away from it: wealth is what most people want from science" (Jevons, 1893, 97). Thus extension of science through practical applications is a way whereby science refreshes and sustains itself. Without extending itself beneficially through the applied sciences, science, that is, pure science, could easily cease to exist.

v. *Although scientists tend to try to verify their hypotheses by designed experiments that are repeatable and repeated, many experiments yield results in terms of probabilities.* When these hypotheses are applied and work successfully in practice, their working provides additional evidence. Thus, for many scientific conclusions, practical application provides a more conclusive kind of conclusion than is otherwise possible. Some scientists seem justified in regarding all practical applications of their conclusions in industry, business, commerce, communications, agriculture, medicine, psychiatry, government, and war, as extensive laboratory experiments supplying additional verificatory evidence. We do not grasp the full nature of science until we become aware of how it becomes verified through the ways in which it behaves in applications.

Distinguishing between science and technology, we can observe that advances in technology "do not form a part of science" (Conant, 1947, 23). "Pure science and technology are not antagonistic but in the long perspective of history reveal themselves to be mutually fructifying, complementary" (Barnett, 1949, 138). As science and technology have become more complicated and more interdependent, some see their interrelationships as more intimate. "The scientist applying his knowledge to the establishment of new or improved products or processes in industry is referred to as a technologist. And so he is but he is not therefore less a scientist than his academically minded brother who abhors industry and all useful arts. The successful scientist must be a competent technologist..." (Hill, 1946, 7).

Rapid extensive industrialization, resulting from science, in turn is having more and more effects on science, effects that may be seen as changing the nature of science itself. "The process of industrialization is irreversible." Science itself has become industrialized. "This thoroughly industrialized science will necessarily become a major part of the scientific enterprise, sharing resources with a few high-prestige fields of 'undirected' research, and allowing some crumbs to the remnants of small-scale individual research" (Ravetz, 1971, 180). Employment of scientists in increasing numbers by government agencies, including legislative committees, to provide assistance needed for making policy decisions, is not only an effect of science but in turn should influence science by stimulating interest in research in new areas where needed knowledge is lacking. When and as the reliability and extensiveness of the social sciences increase, they are likely to make more effective contributions to political, economic, and social policies, and in turn be influenced by financial support.

Evil and dangerous effects of applied science are also a part of what science, in its full sense, is. Atomic bombing of Hiroshima which hastened the end of World War II also had disastrous effects. Responses to these evils, exemplified by establishment of the Federation of Atomic Scientists, the Union of Concerned Scientists, the U.S. Office of Technology Assessment, the International Society for Technology Assessment and its international congresses, and intergovernmental efforts to prevent proliferation of nuclear plants and nuclear bomb production, must be included among the effects of applied science (Baram, 1973, 465-473).

B. Social Effects.

Science is what it does when it behaves in a civilization. Civilizations differ regarding the extent to which and the ways in which science and the sciences have developed and molded other aspects of each civilization. In spite of important discoveries in early Hindu and Chinese civilizations, their cultures have lacked the sustained development in Western civilization resulting from ancient Greek theoretical interests. Although Western civilization has been characterized by the intermingling, sometimes conflicting, of two predominating ideals, one derived from our Greek heritage idealizing reason and one derived from our Hebraic heritage idealizing will (Bahm, 1977a, ch. 3), the progressive advance of science, technology, and industry has gradually reduced the relative importance of Christianity (or of Judaism, Christianity, and Islam) as the dominant cultural determinant. The struggles are not finished, but increasingly even Jewish, Christian, and Islamic combatants depend for success on achieving scientific and technological superiority.

Today division of the world into developed and developing countries results in large part from differences in influences of sciences and technology upon social, economic, political, educational, and health conditions. Science has contributed to both the strengths and weakness of Western civilization. The strengths are well known: increase in wealth, health, longevity, standard of living, and in educational, political, and military power, and now conquests of space. The weaknesses are becoming better known: overpopulation, exhaustion of resources, mechanization of life, pollution, future shock, demoralization. Effects of Hiroshima, megalopolitan pollution, and over-exploitation of natural resources have produced anti-scientific attitudes sufficiently powerful to influence legislative restrictions.

My view is not that we have produced too much science and technology but that production has been imbalanced. What is needed now is more science and more technology, not only in growing numbers of subspecializations, but also in axiology, ethics, religiology, and sociology. This volume is a result of the effects of science, a result of imbalanced effects following from neglect to support and use the value sciences in ways needed to correct the causes of current critical conflicts.[5]

Science behaves in civilizations at large and by "penetration of all aspects of society" (Bronowski, 1956, 710-712). Resisting the temptation to elaborate this claim by illustrating effects in religion, government, education, family life, recreation, and economics, I stop with the remark that all these too are relevant aspects of science.

Summary

Science, fully conceived, includes six components surveyed above: problems, attitude, method, activity, conclusions, and effects. A person may be, and perhaps most scientists are most of the time, scientific in less than the fullest sense. A person aware of a problem as scientific (that is, can be dealt with by means of the scientific attitude and method) is already being scientific, even though dealing with it has not yet begun. Having a scientific attitude is already being scientific that much. A person succeeding in dealing with a particular method in a specialized subscience, even though not understanding the more general nature of science, is still being scientific in a sense. A beginning student in chemistry annealing glass on a first day is already engaged in scientific activity. A person who quotes the conclusions of scientists has appropriated something scientific. Persons who are aware of their lives and desires as shaped by scientific influences have elements of the scientific in them. Each of these minute aspects of science are still aspects of science, and, in a minimal sense, each may be spoken of properly as scientific.

Yet each is so minimal that those engaged occupationally in scientific research are likely to resist such usages as trivial, if not false. But scientific researchers immersed in particular projects often forget that attitude, activity, and effects, and the scientific method in general, are essential to science. The complexity of science in its full sense, to say nothing of the complexities in each specialized context, and the difficulties in keeping all of the six components in mind, contribute to differing emphases in statements about the nature of science. My survey of books and articles on science while preparing this chapter has impressed on me the enormous varieties of views about its nature and the probability that the results of a call on members of the scientific community to state their views on science would be extremely chaotic. Nevertheless, I have faith that scientific problems, attitude, methods, activity, conclusions, and effects exist and can be studied as objectively as other subject matters if we have a genuine willingness to do so. The scientific community has been negligent in requiring reliable research into the science of science (usually called "philosophy of science"). This neglect, too, is part of what science is today.

While this interpretation of science is brief, it should be sufficient to set the stage for any debates about science with those who would define science in such a way as to exclude axiology and other value sciences. Nothing in the nature of science prevents it from including values among the problems investigatable by means of the scientific attitude and method. So I have no hesitancy in requesting members of the scientific community to recognize the existence of axiology as a science.

I am aware that habits of neglect, distrust of what is unfamiliar, and discomfort with challenges to settled convictions, and other obstacles (Bahm, 1974a, ch. 1), are all parts of current science that do inhibit recognition. But I believe that when initial problems are clarified, essential hypotheses formulated, and easily available evidence examined, minds embodying the scientific attitude will be willing to listen, study, and approve recognition of axiology as a science needing urgent attention, support, development, and use.

Three

WHAT ARE VALUES?

Understanding values is complicated because many different kinds of values exist and multitudes of confusions about values, many resulting from false ideas, exist. Sifting through the multifarious kinds of value to find those kinds essential to a sound understanding may seem like a hopeless task to beginners.

But a long history of theoretical controversy has provided literature replete with suggestions. The history of axiology has its own multiplicities of theories. My critical studies during half a century have resulted in an hypothesis, or a complex of hypotheses, about the fundamental kinds of values, in which I have confidence. These hypotheses are proposed here for critical examination by others and for testing in whatever ways are appropriate to their verification.

Twelve kinds of values are distinguished and described in the present chapter. They will be described in six pairs: 1. Good and bad. 2. Ends and means. 3. Subjective and objective values. 4. Apparent and real values. 5. Actual and potential values. 6. Pure and mixed values. A final section will include additional distinctions essential for clarity. These twelve kinds do not exclude each other, for some values embody the essential characteristics of all of the twelve kinds.

1. Good and Bad

The distinction between good and bad is so obvious that I often omit mentioning it. We can safely assume that all adults know how to distinguish between good and bad. Yet the distinction is so fundamental that it is basic to all other discussions about value. Any value theory failing to recognize the distinction between good and bad is not merely inadequate; it is false.

I do not assert that persons distinguishing between good and bad all have the same conceptions of good or bad or of how they are related. Yet some minimum of general statements can be made about good and bad.

A. Good and Bad Are Opposites.

Good is not bad. Bad is not good. Although some persons mistakenly interpret existing opposites as contradictories, good and bad are non-contradictory opposites. Contradictory opposites have nothing in common. Good and bad have something in common. Both are values. Both are alike in being values. Their likeness in being values is inherent in their nature. Thus, good and bad are unlike in some respects and alike in others. Failure to be aware of both the likeness and unlikeness, and failure to distinguish between such likeness and unlikeness, are conducive to confusion and unclear thinking about values.

B. Good and Bad Often Occur as More or Less.

That is, some goods may become more good or less good. Some bads may become more bad or less bad. Although we may be aware of a good or a bad without being aware of it in any sense as more or less, we may also be aware of a good as being more or less good, and of a bad as more or less bad, relative to its earlier or later being, or when compared with another good or bad.

Once comparison begins, we continue to compare, and observe still more good and more bad, and then observe, or wonder, about some most good and most bad. The variable character of goods and bads is embedded in our language in the words "good," "better," "best," and "bad," "worse," and "worst."

When such comparisons are conceived in terms of degrees, then good and bad are conceived as varying by degrees. Conceiving degrees generates the conception of a scale. Unfortunately for simplicity and clarity, many different conceptions of scales, including scales of good and bad, prevail. One conception depicts each degree as being both good and bad, with the degrees at the best end of the scale having progressively less bad while the degrees at the worst end of the scale have progressively less good. A second conception depicts the top quarter of the scale as degrees of good without bad, the bottom quarter of the scale as degrees of bad without good, and the middle half of the scale as degrees differing progressively as more bad and less good, or to reverse the direction, progressively more good and less bad. A third conception depicts a scale ranging in degrees from the most good through the least good, through a midpoint which is neither good nor bad, and then through degrees ranging from the least bad to the most bad. A fourth conception depicts a scale like the third, except that the good and bad ranges are separated by a range that is neither good nor bad.[1] This latter conception raises the question of whether neutral values, values that are neither good nor bad, can exist. Although doubtless some utility can be found for such a conception, especially when values are quantified (just as zero has utility in mathematical scales), I do not propose here as basic to value theory the postulation of neutral values.

I do not propose a theory of degrees or scales as a necessary foundational condition of an adequate theory of values. I have proposed a theory of scales elsewhere (Bahm, 1976, 67-73). This is another problem for scientific investigation, and when reliable conclusions have been demonstrated, the results should serve as useful additions to axiology, that is, to providing a more reliable understanding of good and bad in-so-far as they exist in degrees.

The hypothesis presented here is that, since good and bad do often occur as more or less, our general conceptions of the nature of good and bad should connote such occasional variations.

C. Good and Bad Are Equally Important.

Good and bad are equally important as ingredients in an adequate theory of values. Both good and bad exist. Every person experiences both good and bad. Some persons experience more good than bad during a day, a year, and a lifetime. Probably some persons experience more bad than good during a day, a year, and a lifetime. Persons naturally aim to maximize good and to minimize bad, and, if they are intelligent, to do so on all occasions where they have a choice and sufficient influence. Sometimes expositions of values are facilitated by emphasizing bad. A person may even rightly idealize elimination of all bad and of achieving experience of only good, even only the best. But, since good and bad seem to me to be equally significant constituents of experience, I propose as an hypothesis that they are.[2] I do not say that each life is equally good and bad, but only that good and bad are equally significant as constituents in every life.

2. Ends and Means

A. Why Make the Distinction?

Next to the distinction between good and bad, the distinction between ends and means is the most important distinction necessary for understanding values. Although this distinction is simple enough for everyone to understand, common failure to make the distinction clearly and to keep it in mind when speaking about values is a most prolific source of confusion and misunderstanding.

B. Technical Language.

The meanings of "ends" and "means" interdepend. Means are means to ends. Ends are ends of means. Technical language refers to means as "instrumental values" and to ends as "intrinsic values." Ends, that is, ends-in-themselves, are called intrinsic values because their value is contained within themselves. Means, that is, means to ends-in-themselves, are called instrumental values because their values derive from their usefulness in bringing about or maintaining intrinsic values. If there were no ends-in-themselves there could be no means to them. If, or since, no ends-in-themselves can exist without whatever causes them to exist, there can be no ends without means.

Although instrumental and intrinsic values are two distinguishable and different kinds of value, such that by "instrumental" we do not mean "intrinsic," and by "intrinsic" we do not mean "instrumental," nevertheless some, possibly all, things that have intrinsic value also have instrumental value, and some things that have instrumental value also have intrinsic value. This is another common source of confusion and misunderstanding about values.

C. Instrumental Values.

The value of a thing as instrumental depends upon its bringing about or maintaining some intrinsic value, directly or indirectly. Such "bringing about or maintaining" involves causing or conditioning. That is, things have instrumental value when and because they function causally. Hence, an adequate theory of instrumental value presupposes an adequate theory of causation. I have developed a theory of causation elsewhere (Bahm, 1974b, chs. 19-33). Although I may not be warranted in asserting that axiology as a science must presuppose the principle that "nothing happens without being caused to happen in the way that it does happen," I do make such an assumption and I do include it as a supporting part of my hypothesis about values. All intrinsic values that exist are caused to exist by their causes. All such causes are instrumental values or have instrumental value.

How many kinds of instrumental values are there? As many as there are causes of all of the intrinsic values that exist. If, as seems probable, each thing or event is causally related to all, or most, other things or events in the universe, directly or indirectly, each has a multiplicity of causes. If so, then all of the sciences concerned with understanding any kind of thing, including its causal nature, have something to say that is relevant to instrumental values.

No catalogue of the sciences is presented here. But no science, I believe, escapes dealing with kinds of existences and processes that function, directly or indirectly, in the production of intrinsic values. Hence, axiology as a science depends on all of the other sciences to provide information about instrumental values.

Each intrinsic value is a product of a multiplicity of causes, both a multiplicity of causes functioning simultaneously in bringing it into existence, or maintaining it, and a greater multiplicity of causes functioning serially, since the whole history of causal processes has been involved in the production of those causes operating simultaneously.

D. Intrinsic Value.

The most basic problem of axiology as a general science is to understand intrinsic value. This is its central problem. This is *its* problem. Its other problems relate to, and are generated by, are consequences of, and are implications of, its solution to this problem. Although persons in all other value sciences are also involved, directly or indirectly, with intrinsic values and should understand intrinsic values if they are to deal adequately with their special value problems, the proper locus of the primary investigations into values is axiology. Its problem is a general one, because, although the specialized value sciences deal with special intrinsic values, its central problem is to understand intrinsic value itself.

My task here as axiologist is to clarify and define the problem, to make appropriate observations about the problem that will lead to the formulation of an hypothesis, and then to test the hypothesis. The present chapter is devoted primarily to the formulation of an hypothesis. Questions pertaining to testing will be treated in chapter Five.

i. *My hypothesis: Historical background.* In formulating my hypothesis, I have drawn on four historically prominent theories as contributing parts. The early formulation and historical endurance of these four theories are evidence that they have located something necessary for value theory. But I have also tested the proposal by extensive observations of my experiences. I have deliberately sought a fifth kind of intrinsic value and have tried out such a fifth in a working hypothesis. My present knowledge warrants postulating that there are only four. I have also tried out the hypothesis on my students during many years. But the hypothesis is one that you can test for yourself if you are willing to attend to needed observations.

A part of the hypothesis is that there are four distinguishable kinds of intrinsic values. How they interdepend, supplement each other, and blend into each other, I discuss later. The first task is to sharpen their distinctions by showing how each of the four has been the primary, and often exclusive, kind of intrinsic value claimed as ultimate by each of the four theories. The theories are quite well known, although persons subscribing to one of them tend to ignore and deny the others. I use names associated with their technical history, some less well known than others.

(1) *The four theories* are named "Hedonism," "Voluntarism," "Romanticism," and "Anandism." Each may be stated simply, both as a theory of goodness and as a theory of badness.

(a) *Hedonism.* According to Hedonism, intrinsic good consists in pleasant feeling while intrinsic bad consists in unpleasant feeling, pain being the obvious example of unpleasant feeling. The key idea of early Hedonists is sensory pleasure, exemplified in sweet flavors, fragrant odors, bright colors, dulcet tones, soft, smooth, and warm feelings, and even tickling sensations. Intrinsic evil is also primarily sensory, exemplified by bitter flavors, foul odors, dull colors, screechy sounds, hard, rough, and hot feelings, and even itchy sensations. As long as you are enjoying a pleasant feeling, intrinsic good exists in your experience. As long as you are suffering an unpleasant feeling, intrinsic bad exists in your experience. Such feelings are present in awareness and are intuited as ends-in-themselves. Pleasant feelings are good-in-themselves. Unpleasant feelings are bad-in-themselves.

Sensations, whether pleasant or unpleasant, may vary in intensity and duration, thereby increasing or decreasing actual intrinsic good or evil. Hedonistic axiology serves as a basis for Hedonistic ethics: a person ought to act in such a way as to try to maximize pleasant feelings and to minimize unpleasant feelings.

Hedonism involves a paradox, traditionally known as "the Hedonistic Paradox." When you seek pleasant feelings directly, you do not find them. In order to attain pleasant feelings, you must engage in activities that produce them as a consequence. You do not find enjoyment of sweetness merely by desiring to enjoy sweetness. You must engage in some activity, such as growing sugar cane, purchasing sugar, making candy, and eating candy. Because this is so, we often unconsciously locate the sweetness in the candy and automatically locate the enjoyed intrinsic value in it also. But the candy, and other contributions, are instrumental values, or means to the enjoyment. This paradox is another source of confusion in thinking about values.

When critics denounced Hedonism as a "pig philosophy," because pigs and other animals enjoy sensory pleasures and suffer sensory pains, some Hedonists extended the meaning of pleasant feelings to include "qualities." Once expansion of the meaning of pleasure had begun, it was extended to "pleasures of the intellect," including feelings experienced in enjoying poetry, symphonic music, and even mathematical calculations. But the sensory origins of Hedonistic ideas often lingered in linguistic expressions, such as "sweet music," "sour note," "bitter argument," and "foul play."

(b) *Voluntarism*. According to Voluntarism, intrinsic good consists in feeling satisfaction of desire while intrinsic bad consists in feeling frustrated. The key idea combines desire and satisfaction. Without desire, there can be no satisfaction. Not the desire but the feeling of satisfaction is experienced as intrinsically good. This feeling is most obvious while desire is being satisfied, though a person may retain awareness of a desire having been satisfied, that is, a continuing feeling of satisfaction. Without desire, we can have no frustration. Not the desire but the feeling of desire being frustrated is experienced as intrinsically bad. This feeling is most obvious while the desire is being frustrated, though a person may retain an awareness of a desire having been frustrated, or a continuing feeling of frustration.

Feelings of satisfaction and frustration may vary in intensity and duration. Desires vary in intensity, so more intense desires tend to result in more intense feelings when being satisfied or frustrated. A more intense feeling of satisfaction is intuited as intrinsically more good. A more intense feeling of frustration is intuited as intrinsically more bad. Although sometimes long-standing desires are felt as being satisfied or frustrated only briefly, and sometimes suddenly originating desires are felt as being satisfied or frustrated for a long time, long-standing desires often result in enduring feelings of satisfaction or frustration. In any case, when a feeling of satisfaction is prolonged, intuited intrinsic value increases through such prolongation, and when a feeling of frustration is prolonged, intuited intrinsic evil increases proportionately. Voluntaristic axiology is the basis for voluntaristic ethics: you ought to act in such a way as to maximize feelings of satisfaction and to minimize feelings of frustration.

Voluntarism involves a paradox. Although intrinsic good is held to exist as the feeling of satisfaction, it often appears as if located in the object or objective desired. You do not normally consciously desire a feeling of satisfaction. You thirst, and drinking satisfies your desire by slaking your thirst. You desire to possess, and feel satisfied by attaining. You desire to go, and feel satisfied as you begin to move. Satisfaction comes from having desires for particular things, objects, activities, achievements. So attention is focused on such things. They become inherent parts of (or the whole of) the goal sought. Then the intrinsic good sought often appears as if located in them. The paradox may be stated in another way: Although things are good (instrumentally) because we desire them, nevertheless we seem to desire them because they appear to be good (instrumentally). Voluntarism as a philosophy is conducive to preoccupation with the acquisition of things, instruments, and means for facilitating satisfactions.

The same is true of feelings of frustration. Although the Voluntarist does not seek to have desires frustrated, they are frustrated by some thing, object, activity, or failure, so the intrinsic evil experiences are located as if in the thing. This paradox also causes confusion when thinking about values.

(c) *Romanticism*. According to Romanticism, intrinsic good consists in feelings of desirousness, exemplified in feelings of eagerness, enthusiasm, exuberance, excitement, zest, gusto, avidity, hope, longing, fervor, passion, lust, and even anger and rage. Intrinsic value is located not in the satisfaction but in the desiring. In fact, satisfaction, because it terminates desiring, destroys enjoyment of desiring and thus eliminates it as intrinsic value. Frustration, when it arouses feelings of resentment, anger, and a stronger desire to overcome what causes the frustration, thus increases desirousness, and thereby increases intrinsic goodness. Intrinsic evil, according to Romanticism, consists not in feelings of frustration but in feelings of apathy. When desire subsides, desirousness disappears. No desire, no desirousness; no desirousness, no enjoyment of intrinsic value. Both physiological weakness and environmental affluence causing desires to be too easily satisfied militate against maintaining desirousness.

Desirousness and apathy vary in intensity and duration. Enthusiasm, eagerness, anticipation, excitement all occur in degrees. For the Romanticist, the greater the enthusiasm, as more intense and more prolonged, the greater the intrinsic value enjoyed. Romanticistic axiology provides a basis for Romanticistic ethics: A person ought to act so as to maximize desirousness and to minimize apathy. But practicing Romanticists experience peaks of elation and pits of depression because body vitality, even in vigorous youths, and the many different kinds of activities through which desires can be intensified and prolonged have limits. Although persons in environments rich in resources may not reach such limits as quickly as those who are weak, poor or rural, all do reach them.

Intrinsic evil exists when you feel deprived of desirousness. As soon as you experience a diminution of intensity, a retreat from the peak of intensity, you may become aware of growing deprivation.[3] Some Romanticists sink rapidly from peak to pit; others manage to prolong the decline. Awareness of absence of interesting things to do is often experienced as boredom. You may think of boredom as the opposite of enthusiasm. This is only partly true, for as long as you feel bored, you retain a feeling of annoyance which has a desire to be relieved from the boredom implicit in it; sometimes boredom expresses itself through violent language or other minor violent actions. The ultimate intrinsic evil is the feeling of apathy, of utter desirelessness, even without any concern about whether desire returns again. You may be more or less bored and more or less apathetic. The more completely apathetic you feel and the more prolonged such feelings of apathy, the greater the amount of intrinsic evil experienced.

Romanticism involves another paradox. It shares the Voluntaristic paradox of desiring objects seeming to be the loci of intrinsic value even though the intrinsic value exists actually in the felt desire. But it involves the additional paradox of eulogizing desires which by nature aim to become fulfilled in satisfaction, thereby locating intrinsic value in such satisfaction, but then claiming that intrinsic value is to be found in desiring rather than in satisfaction. It bolsters its claim by showing that satisfaction kills desires whereas frustration intensifies desires. And it demonstrates its claim by observing its own primary data, enjoyment of feelings of enthusiasm, intuited as ends-in-themselves as obviously as feelings of pleasure or satisfaction. These paradoxes and the evidence for them function as additional causes of confusion regarding values.[4]

(d) *Anandism*. "Anandism" is the name I give to the ancient and contemporary Hindu view that intrinsic good consists in intuited enjoyment of feeling completely contented (*ananda*, bliss) and that intrinsic bad consists in feeling disturbed, and thus robbed of such contentment. Desire, which is the locus of intrinsic value for both Voluntarism and Romanticism, is regarded as the source of all evil (instrumentally) and as the embodiment of intrinsic evil. As long as you desire, your perfect tranquility is disturbed.

Although Anandism is least familiar to Western minds, its prevalence for millennia attests to its significance and, even though we may not accept its ideals stated in extreme form, its claim about intrinsic value refers to something naturally present in the experiences of every person that can be intuited as intrinsic good whenever observed. Hindus have idealized perfection as involving pure, undifferentiated, quiescent being (*sat*), pure, completely vacuous, quiescent awareness (*chit*), and pure, undisturbed, quiescent bliss (*ananda*). *Sat-chit-ananda*, ultimate reality, knowledge and value, is viewed as perfect tranquility of being, awareness, and enjoyment. The Hindu conception of pure intrinsic good, undisturbed quietude, is also named *Nirvana*, "no wind."

Whatever disturbs this quietude is evil. Hence, pleasures as well as pains, satisfactions as well as desires and frustrations, eagerness, ambition, zeal, anxiety, and yearning, as well as annoying apathy, all exist as disturbances of placidity, and thereby are experienced as intrinsic evil.

Although the Hindu ideal of Nirvana is conceived as attainable by only a few in this life (*jivanmukti*), the enjoyment of rest is something experienced by every human being. Strictly speaking, no degrees of Nirvana can exist, but the contentment experienced by human beings may appear as more and less. Depth psychology reveals levels of contentment, so that you may suffer deep-seated disturbance while enjoying surface calm, or you may enjoy deeply-enduring contentment while grappling constantly with violent challenges of daily turmoil. Zen's spontaneously yea-saying attitude toward whatever problems appear exemplifies depth contentment as a means for dealing with surface troubles (Bahm, 1964, 206-221).

Anandistic axiology provides a foundation for Anandistic ethics: You should try to act in such a way that you will eventually eliminate all action by desiring to eliminate all desire, and, in the meantime, to eliminate as much action, and desire, as you can. The need for seeking attainment of contentment, the intrinsic value, within life is amply illustrated and explained in Hindu literature. Yogic devotees are advised to abandon ambition and to accept daily and moral responsibilities unquestioningly. Although many different yogas (ways) are available, through all you should practice *nishkama* yoga, proceeding "without desire" (Bahm, 1970, 5-16). Then you will embody that "action which is in inaction" and that "inaction which is in action" (Bahm, 1970, 46). Anandism's paradox of paradoxes centers around the need for desiring desirelessness. "The desire of the mind to suppress disturbances is itself a disturbance of the mind which must also be suppressed before it can reach the state in which desire is completely suppressed" (Patanjali, 1961, 126). Although paradoxical explanations yield confused thinking about values, the yielding to uncritical enjoyment of contentment provides intuitive apprehension of intrinsic value that defies description.

(2) *Their differences*. Differences in the four theories have bases in differences between the four kinds of values. How do pleasure, satisfaction, eagerness, and contentment differ? How do pain, frustration, apathy, and anxiety differ? Differences between the theories may be clarified by focusing on differences between the values denoted as typical or archetypal by each theory.

Pleasure, or pleasant feeling, occurs obviously as pleasing sensation, such as a sweet flavor, fragrant odor or bright color. Unpleasant feeling appears obviously in pain sensation, such as that accompanying a cut, bump, or ache. Sensory pleasures and pains may appear in awareness without having been desired. When a sweet flavor occurs in awareness, it may generate a desire for its continuance or for another. When a pain occurs in awareness, it may generate a desire for its cessation and for non-recurrence. But the presence of desire is not essential for the appearances of pleasures and pains.

Satisfaction on the other hand does require desire as a condition of its existence. Frustration also does. Desire involves volition and intention. Whereas sensory pleasures and pains may be simply presented, often appearing as pleasing or unpleasant objects, desires emerge from the self. Although desires tend to objectify themselves in the form of objects desired or objectives sought, desires are experienced as wants or lacks that need to be filled. Whereas sensations typically begin as presentations, desires typically begin as awareness of absence. Satisfaction is experienced as filling that lack. Both negative absence or want and a positive presence of what fulfills that want are required for the existence of a feeling of satisfaction. Frustration is experienced as intensification of want after effort to satisfy, or expectation of satisfaction.

Eagerness also presupposes desire but not satisfaction. Apathy presupposes desire and awareness of its absence. Whereas frustration involves lack of satisfaction, apathy involves lack of desire. Typically, desirousness occurs as eagerness, enthusiasm, exuberance, excitement, zeal, and thrill. Typically, apathy appears in feelings of exhaustion, abandonment of struggle, and stupor. Eagerness is future-oriented, and is often felt as having an indefinite, perhaps infinite, future. Whereas satisfaction is felt as terminal or as terminating, a feeling of enthusiasm does not imply intention to terminate. When a person is most enthusiastic, enthusiasm seems interminable. It inspires some to sing about "reaching for the unreachable stars." Sentimentalists describe it as "infinite longing."

Contentment as an ideal presupposes not desire but complete absence of desire. Yet since the only way human beings experience contentment is through achieving it by having desire, then satisfaction, and then cessation of the desire, human contentment also presupposes desire. But since desire itself disturbs peaceful quiescence, it functions as an intrinsic evil that needs to be overcome. The quantities of sedatives sold are evidence of the magnitude of desires for undisturbed (desireless) sleep. Satisfaction, on the one hand, is a feeling of fulfillment of desire in which the desire being fulfilled continues to be present as an ingredient in the feeling of satisfaction. Contentment, on the other hand, is a feeling of fullness, enoughness, or sufficiency, without concern for what, if any, desire has been fulfilled. Genuine contentment is a general feeling, not something related to any particular desires or satisfactions. Complete contentment is not experienced as something that was anticipated. Although experience contains events that come and go, contentment as a feeling transcends these events and remains unconcerned about them. They may be experienced as presented, but the feeling of contentment is experienced merely as present.

(3) *Exclusive claims.* Ardent advocates of each of the four theories claim that the intrinsic value upon which it focuses is the only ultimate kind of intrinsic value. Each such claim aims to exclude all of the others from ultimacy or equal ultimacy. Each tries to include all of the other values within itself in subordinate ways. It does this by interpreting the other values as reducible to, explainable in terms of, or as inferior to, its kind of value. Observing how each states its claims may reveal more about values as well as about the theories.

(a) Hedonists, beginning with pleasant sensation, first extended durationally, next intentionally, then qualitatively, employ the vaguer and more general term "pleasant feeling" to include enjoyments felt as satisfactions, enthusiasms, and contentment. Pain, bitter taste, foul odors, etc., are clearly sensuous, but the word "unpleasant feeling" can be extended to include feelings of frustration, apathy, and anxiety. Then, the Hedonist will claim that "pleasure is the only good" because "pleasant feeling" is a most general term for enjoyment. The words employed by Voluntarism, Romanticism, and Anandism are regarded as specific kinds of pleasant feeling. Hence each is inadequate because it ignores the intuited intrinsic goodness of sensory pleasures and the intuited evil of sensory pains.

(b) Voluntarists, distinguishing between pleasing sensation and satisfaction, regard the former as a presented stimulus which does not really yield pleasure until desire to enjoy it arises. A person may be aware of flavors, odors, colors, and other sensations without either liking or disliking them. But when a person responds to experienced sensation with interest and an attitude of appreciation, that is, with desire, then they become values, not before. The human body is so adapted, as a consequence of biological evolution, that it sometimes

reacts automatically to some stimuli with arousal of desire. Relative
to some things, especially those needed for survival, the body has built-
in, latent, desires that become aroused automatically with sensory
stimulation.   But it is the desire, with its feeling of actual or
anticipatory satisfaction, that is the locus of intrinsic value, not the
bare sensation itself.

Voluntarists explain eagerness as merely a form of desire with
heightened intensity.   Greater eagerness or desirousness is a
manifestation of a greater or deeper or more lasting satisfaction
sought. To locate intrinsic value in desiring rather than in satisfaction
constitutes perversion. Romanticists emulate wild animals, such as
those that prance about violently without knowing where they are
going. Satisfaction alone is the ultimate good, and eagerness, zeal or
enthusiasm function as anticipatory satisfaction in proportion to the
intensity of the feeling of satisfaction expected. Contentment, too, is
really a state of satisfied desire.   Although Anandists pretend to
idealize contentment isolated from desire, this is an unrealistic analysis,
as they themselves admit; for contentment as restfulness, peace, or
repose implies a desire to have quit restlessness, war, or agitation.
Unpleasant sensation results from automatic responses which desire
the absence of such sensation and is felt as frustration of such desire
as long as the unpleasant feeling persists. Apathy is really a feeling of
general exhaustion or lack of desire for activity. Anxiety is felt as evil
only when one desires its absence; only then is its continued presence
felt as frustrating.

(c) Romanticists, accepting Voluntarism's criticisms of Hedonism,
condemn Voluntarism's location of intrinsic value in satisfaction as
deadening. Life, vivacity, vitality consist in exertion of will, not in its
cessation, in the urgency of desire, not in its subsidence, in the
continuing intensity of impulsiveness, not in its exhaustion. To become
satisfied is to become apathetic, indifferent, torpid, dead. Romanticists
not only agree with voluntarism's criticism of Anandism, but regard
perfect contentment as the worst of all evils.   Animals that are
perfectly contented, no matter what happens to them, soon get eaten;
survival depends on fighting and on emotions heightened as fear,
anger, jealousy, rage, and greed. Feelings of vigor and enthusiasm are
needed for survival. These, not satisfaction or contentment, constitute
biologically-established intrinsic value. Unpleasant sensations, such as
pain, bitter flavors and foul odors, and frustrations and anxiety keep us

concerned and invigorated. Hence, they are not evils, as Hedonism, Voluntarism and Anandism claim. Instead, they are varieties of goods that keep us aroused and active. Although boredom may be felt as negative, the real evil is apathy or contentment; for as long as you feel bored, you retain an interest in vitality, whereas when you become satisfied, contented or apathetic, your life and its intrinsic value are gone.

(d) Anandists reject all views holding that intrinsic value consists ultimately in pleasant sensations, satisfactions, and enthusiasms. Although these may serve as temporary values that arouse interest in, and help to show the way toward, contentment, they are not, in themselves, ultimate. As long as they disturb enjoyment of peace and quietude by calling attention to themselves, they are evils. Pain, frustration, and apathy are also evils, but hardly more so, for all function as forms or manifestations of desire which alone is the ultimate source of evil. Pleasures are evil because they arouse desire for more. Desires are evil because they lead to frustrations which intensify desires or to satisfactions which persist as tendencies to arouse desire for more of the same. Eagerness or desirousness is simply desire at its most intense, hence worst, form. Romanticism and Anandism agree that each is the other's worst enemy, though Hedonism may be more subtly inimical because less obviously opposed to Anandism. Not even satisfaction is good as long as it remains infected with traces of the desire being satisfied.

ii. *My hypothesis: Debts to the four theories.* My hypotheses about values is indebted to the four theories summarized. I recognize that each theory has located a genuine and distinguishable kind of intrinsic value, both intrinsically good and intrinsically bad. I also reject the negative claims in each theory when each denies ultimacy, or equal ultimacy, to the values emphasized by the other theories.

The following comparative diagram may help to depict the four theories and the four kinds of intrinsic value.

iii. *My hypothesis: Additional observations*: Some further observations about the four kinds of values seem in order before formulating my theory.

(1) Similarities. Despite their differences, both actual and those magnified by competing theorists, pleasure, satisfaction, enthusiasm, and contentment, and pain, frustration, apathy, and disturbance, are all alike in several respects.

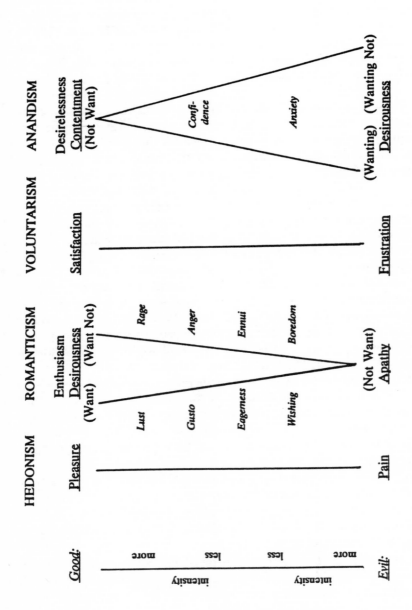

DIAGRAM

Four theories (kinds) of intrinsic value (good and evil).

(a) All occur in awareness. They appear, vaguely or clearly. They may exist conceptualized (for example, as ingredient in a perceived object, a merry party, a religious doctrine, or a life plan), or they may appear as unconceptualizable. Instrumental values may exist without awareness. But intrinsic value itself, all four theories agree, must be experienced in order to be.

(b) All are intuited. Each is directly apprehended. No one needs any proof of its existence because it is self-evident, and self-evidently good, or bad, while it is being experienced. You may ignore it when focusing attention on other aspects of a complex experience. You may even have adopted or developed an ideology establishing a mind-set habitually ignoring some intuitable values. But when present in awareness and in attention, each can be enjoyed intuitively, with or without conceptualization.

(c) All may occur variably. I do not mean that on every occurrence each varies while being attended to, but that all of the eight kinds of value differ from time to time as well as often being experienced as varying during one act of awareness. Pleasures and pains, satisfactions and frustrations, enthusiasms and apathies, and contentment and disturbances may vary as more and less. Each may become more and less intense and more and less enduring. Each may also differ in quality, though I have difficulty describing what is meant by quality, and each of the kinds of intrinsic value will have its kinds of quality. Some qualities result from associations with concepts and contexts, so I prefer to defer to further research details of how these different kinds of intrinsic value differ in quality.

(d) All are "felt" and either "enjoyed" or "suffered." All intrinsic values are feelings: pleasant and unpleasant feelings, feelings of satisfaction and frustration, feelings of eagerness and apathy, feelings of contentment and disturbance. All intrinsic goods are enjoyed. All intrinsic bads are suffered. I am not sure that "enjoyed" and "suffered" are the best words to denote what is common to all good and bad feelings; I welcome suggestions for improvement. For the present, I propose using "enjoyed" and "suffered" to name how all good feelings and all bad feelings have in common are experienced.

(e) All have biological bases. All of these intrinsic values appear to have evolved in, and to continue to depend upon, the biological and physiological natures of human beings. How each kind of sensory end organ, each kind of glandular secretion, each bone and muscle, each neural and brain response evolved is a long and complicated story. Uniformities in kinds of intrinsic values felt by all human beings depend on biological and physiological uniformities. Doubtless some individual and racial variations exist in biological and physiological conditions that result in differing qualities of feelings. Comparative deficiencies in olfactory acuity, for example, can affect the qualities of value experiences. But, except for deviances regarded as abnormal, such as blindness and deafness, all human beings have a minimum of common conditions sufficient to warrant universal generalizations about the feelings involved in these four, or eight, kinds of intrinsic values.

(f) All may appear paradoxical. Each of the four theories involves a central paradox. Hedonism: pleasure-seekers find pleasure not by seeking pleasure but by pursuing other activities that yield pleasure as an accompaniment. Voluntarism: persons find satisfaction by projecting objects or objectives appearing as the goods desired and then achieving them, even though the intrinsic value sought in desiring is in satisfaction and not in the objects. Romanticism: (although accepting desire, which is, by nature, desire for satisfaction, as the location of intrinsic value) persons locate intrinsic value in desirousness and condemn satisfaction as extinction of desire. Anandism: seekers can find contentment only by desiring desirelessness. Each of the four values may be achievable at times only through awareness of such paradoxical seeking.

All of the foregoing six similarities are conceived as inherent in intrinsic value as proposed in my hypothesis.

(2) Supplementarities. The four kinds of intrinsic value are similar in many ways and also supplementary in several ways.

(a) Each kind supplies something that the others lack in constituting all experienced intrinsic value. I propose that an adequate account of intrinsic value must include all of the four. Each has a contribution to make, and thus supplements and is supplemented by the others in a complete account.

(b) Each kind of intrinsic value is variable. There may be more or less of it. Each may endure longer or shorter, may be more and less intense, may be more and less recurrent, and, what interests us here, may more fully and less fully occupy awareness. Each may fully occupy awareness. Each may be entirely absent from attention. Each may occur together with one or all of the others, in one act of awareness or in rapid succession, usually conditioned by perceptual and conceptual factors. When they exist together it is sometimes possible to distinguish them. But more often each blends into the others so that distinctions become unobservable. In such blends, sometimes one and sometimes another kind will dominate. Thus, the four kinds supplement each other by constituting experienced intrinsic value in these varying ways.

(c) Intrinsic values may be observed to supplement each other successively, in constituting a rapid series of stages in some complex value experiences as well as in predominating differentially in the major stages of normal life cycles.

Moderate succession of the four kinds may be observed during normal coital experience. Pleasant feelings originating when erogenous zones are stimulated often initiate desire, which then becomes aroused and grows in intensity to passionate impetuosity, which is followed by an orgasmic climax experienced as intensely satisfying, which then subsides into a feeling of contentment so complete that even all of the previous feelings have been forgotten.

Much slower, and much less easily observable without considerable memory and inferential generalization, is an apparent succession of the dominance of each of the four kinds of value during four successive stages in normal life cycles. Infants and children are more preoccupied with sensory pleasures and pains. Although they often express violent exuberance and often sleep contentedly, they are more easily disturbed by and pacified by sensory pains and pleasures. Youth is a time of energy and enthusiasm. Youth is desirous and ambitious, and not easily satisfied with anything. Youths often express desires more vigorously, more wistfully, more longingly, even more violently. Youths are more impatient with apathy. Adults become preoccupied with achieving the goals of life and with recognizing the extent to which such goals are being attained. Thus adults strive for feelings of satisfaction. The aged spend more time enjoying contentment, because vitality diminishes, energy declines, insensitivity progresses, and achievable goals of life have been accomplished. Pleasures and pains, desirousness and apathy, satisfaction and frustration, and contentment and annoyance occur plentifully during all stages and all ages of life. But infancy, youth, adulthood, and old age are more preoccupied more by each of the four.[11]

(3) Interdependence. Each kind depends on all of the others to

supplement it in constituting all intrinsic value, and each influences the others in numerous ways.

Although you may contemplate and enjoy sensory experiences without having desire aroused to continue or repeat the experience, normally pleasant sensation arouses desire and bestirs appropriate body mechanisms, especially when the sensations are intense. Sensation and desire interdepend instrumentally in that sensation is required for the arousal of some desires and some sensations will occur only because desire to attain them exists. Repeated sensory enjoyments resulting in recurrent desires establish habits generating recurrent desires.

Although sensations may arouse desires and desires may arouse sensations, desire may be aroused without significant awareness of sensation. Sometimes bodily energy becomes superabundant and manifests itself spontaneously as desire for activity. You may experience a burgeoning of desire before projecting conceptually something desired. You may enjoy desiring without knowing what you desire or what will serve to satisfy your desire. Although developed persons normally are so conditioned with profusions of ideas that ideation is automatic when desires emerge from superabundant energy, generally the feeling of desire is prior to ideation about specific goals that can satisfy desire. Even adults may become restless and express desire to act without having clear ideas about what they want to do. On the other hand, ideas of what you need generate desires for them and consequently do generate any desirousness needed to activate efforts to achieve satisfaction.

Satisfaction depends on desire, but desire also depends on satisfaction, for if desires were never satisfied, they would soon cease to exist. Satisfaction of desire generates more desire for more satisfaction. The more different kinds of ideas you can employ in formulating the objects or objectives of desire, the more desires will be stimulated.

When satisfaction so fulfills a desire that the desire itself is terminated, a person feels contented. Contentment depends upon both desire and satisfaction for its coming into existence. But does contentment, absence of desire, cause desire? Although interdependence of feelings and physiological conditions characterize all four kinds of intrinsic values, the ways in which other values depend on contentment is more dependent on such conditions. Although exhausting energy-consuming activity itself generates desire for contentment, perfect contentment has no way of generating desire. After contentment has persisted so that body energy becomes replenished and expansively calls for expression, desires become aroused. Contentment is then instrumental in enabling needed rest required for replenishment of the energy needed by desires.

Although our concern here is primarily with how the four kinds of intrinsic values interdepend, their interdependence with instrumental values, with biological, physiological, physical, chemical, ecological, social, cultural, and other of factors, cannot be overstressed. The factors examined in dealing with ends and means interdepend with the factors involved in actual-versus-potential, subjective-versus-objective, and apparent-versus-real values, even though I will not explore all of them in this volume.

The similarities, supplementarities (including variabilities, varieties of blending, and variations in dominance and subordination), and interdependencies of the four kinds of value are additional sources of popular confusion about values.

iv. *My hypothesis: Beginning formulation.* Intrinsic value consists in feelings of enjoyment and suffering distinguishable into four kinds that may be called (1) pleasant and unpleasant feelings, (2) feelings of satisfaction and frustration, (3) feelings of desirousness and apathy, and (4) feelings of contentment and disturbance. These four kinds are alike in occurring in awareness, in being intuited, in occurring variably, in being felt, that is, enjoyed or suffered, in having biological bases, and in appearing sometimes as paradoxical to seekers. The four supplement each other and interdepend in constituting experienced intrinsic value. Intrinsic value and instrumental value also interdepend, as previously noted. The foregoing is part of my hypothesis about the nature of values, that is, that part pertaining to ends and means, or intrinsic and instrumental goods and bads.

3. Actual and Potential Values

A. All Feelings Are Temporal and Temporary.

Intrinsic value consists in feelings actually enjoyed and suffered. Thus, all actual intrinsic values are temporal and temporary. How temporary?

The answer to this question involves answers to questions about how long is the present, that is, actual, experience, and thus to questions about time. Axiology depends upon information provided by metaphysicians, physicists, physiologists, and physiological psychologists about time, temporal processes, and present experience.

Detailed exploration of the nature of time is omitted here (Bahm, 1974b, ch. 11). But some understanding of present experience is necessary for understanding intrinsic values. Whether there is any way in which actual intrinsic value exists beyond present awareness is a question that I defer to further research. For present purposes, intrinsic values exist only in present awareness.

How long is present awareness? A precise answer is difficult to give because awarenesses differ in length. When you are very alert, your present awareness is longer than when you are drowsy. Awareness exists in pulses with gaps of unawareness between them. Imagine a horizontal series of similar waves, with a line drawn through them near the tops of the waves. The length of each wave above the line is shorter than the length between each wave at that level. Drowsy awareness is depicted as short pulses of awareness with longer periods of unawareness between them. Now draw a line through the waves near the bottoms of the waves. The length of each wave above this line is longer than the length between each wave at that level. Alert awareness is depicted as longer pulses of awareness with shorter periods of unawareness between them.

These simplified examples illustrate how present awarenesses differ in length. They also exemplify the fact that awarenesses are discrete even though you are not aware of the gaps. Absence of awareness of unawareness leaves the impression of continuous awareness. Indirect evidence of how long a present awareness lasts may be observed in eye jerks. Observe another person reading. The line being read, and the reading of the line, appear to be continuous. But you can observe that eyes stop and jump, stop and jump, repeatedly. Other evidence comes from movies, where pictures on films must stop and move fast enough so that the projected pictures will seem continuous to observers. Experimental evidence about lengths of pulses of awareness and gaps between them has been well documented.

Two implications of these facts for value theory may be noted. First, intrinsic value exists actually only in or during pulses of awareness. When you are more alert, you enjoy or suffer more intrinsic value. When you are less alert, you enjoy or suffer less intrinsic value. However, since enjoyment of feelings often appears to continue for longer periods, it appears that, somehow, vigorously alert minds are able to intuitively apprehend continuity of feelings over longer periods than single pulses of attention. Whether such acts of attention involve more extensive pulses of awareness or whether an emergent mind has a continuity of its own over and above normal pulses of awareness is something I defer to further research. But actual intrinsic values are clearly temporal and temporary, even if we have not yet reached final conclusions about how long a particular actual intrinsic value may last.

Second, intrinsic value, like other aspects of experience, including concepts, depends continuingly on multiplicities of complex and intricately interrelated causal conditions that make feelings and pulses of awareness possible. These other aspects, also temporal, each involving its kind of temporal units and actual presents, cause and support such awareness and feelings. Although awareness and feelings seem more dependent on their supporting conditions than those supporting conditions depend on awareness and feelings, nevertheless evidence, such as the permanent obstruction of vision that results in deterioration of supporting cells, indicates that active functioning of awareness and feelings are necessary for their health. Thus, the existence of some intrinsic value is essential for the existence of human beings. The human body depends on minimal actualization of intrinsic value.

B. All Feelings Are Caused.

Thus all intrinsic values are caused. I propose a completely deterministic hypothesis that all intrinsic values are caused to occur in the way that they do occur (Bahm, 1974b, chs. 19-32). All of the causes and conditions of the occurrence of intrinsic values are called instrumental values. Some of these are quite general; for example, those sustaining the earth, without which an earth-dweller's feelings would not exist. Some are more specific; for example, those pertaining to causing olfactory, gustatory, or visual sensations, including the kinds of things producing sensory feelings. Some are more particular; for example, the chemicals constituting the sugar now stimulating my taste buds and the electro-chemical factors producing nerve impulses resulting in my awareness of sweetness. All of the causes, general, specific, and particular, of an actual value are instrumental values relative to it. The actualization of actual intrinsic value automatically actualizes the causing instruments to be actual instrumental values.

But what about potential intrinsic and potential instrumental values? The causes of actual intrinsic value had the power to cause it. Otherwise they could not have caused it. Such power, or potency, is called "potential" before the power results in actualization. Thus, we speak of such power, potency, or potentiality of the causes instrumental within producing actual intrinsic value as having "potential value."

Although intrinsic values do not exist actually before they actually exist, most of the powers producing them do exist actually before the intrinsic values actually exist. But we do not call these things actual instrumental values until the actual intrinsic value exists. Yet they have natures such that they are enabled, cooperatively, to cause such values. The natures of some of the things that cause intrinsic values can function without causing intrinsic values to exist.

Take as example, two ears of corn, one of which, when eaten, causes enjoyment, and the other of which is not eaten and does not cause enjoyment. Both are actual ears of corn. Both have natures such that, if and when eaten, they can contribute to causing enjoyment. In the way that both have the power to contribute to causing enjoyment, provided all other needed causes cooperate, they may be thought of as having potential value. Spare parts manufactured to repair obsolete automobiles are such that, although all could be used to actualize repairs if selected for use, some are selected, while some are not.

Before a thing actually causes intrinsic value, we an speak of it as having "conditional potential instrumental value." The conception of conditional potential instrumental value is useful not only for understanding value theory in general but also because most things have multiplicities of such conditional potential values and many of the obligations people have, as persons or as manufacturers, pertain primarily to such values. They function as bases for conditional oughts, a most common kind of ought, as I explain in *Ethics: The Science of Oughtness*, chapter 2.

Understanding the natures of all things that can function as conditional potential instrumental value is the task of all of the sciences. Thus, axiology depends on all of the sciences for providing such understanding. Such understanding becomes a part of axiology to the extent that it is needed for, and is appropriated for, understanding the different kinds of causes of the different kinds of value.

What about potential intrinsic values? We may construct ideas of, and ideals about, intrinsic values existing potentially prior to their actuality. These may have some pragmatic usefulness for practical purposes. But as far as foundational theory is concerned, I see no need for postulating the existence of potential intrinsic values. The actualization of any intrinsic value requires all of the multiplicity of causes (conditional potential instrumental values), and the actual intrinsic value does not exist even potentially in any one of them, or in all of them together.

There is one exception to this generalization. Each actual intrinsic value may function also instrumentally in causing another intrinsic value. Insofar as the caused intrinsic value is different from what caused it, it can hardly have existed as potential intrinsic value in the actual intrinsic value that (partly) caused it. But insofar as the caused intrinsic value is like, or is the same as, the intrinsic value which caused it, some kind of potential intrinsic value may be recognized to have existed in the causing intrinsic value. For, in spite of the discreetness of successive pulses of awareness and enjoyment, the enjoyment appears as actually continuous; and in such apparently continuous enjoyment, what precedes has an actual intrinsic value which is part of the power, or potentiality, involved in causing its apparent continuation and actual enjoyment. Such power is intrinsic value as potential, and to the extent that it is experienced as continuing in an experience, it functions as potential intrinsic value.

C. My Hypothesis About the Nature of Values Includes an Hypothesis About Actual and Potential Values.

Intrinsic values are temporal and temporary, and exist actually only in and during pulses of awareness or in and during any continuing (non-discontinuous) awareness made possible by emergent mind intuitively apprehending as actually present durations inclusive of more than one normal pulse of awareness. Intrinsic value are caused. All of the causes of an actual intrinsic value include some that are general, some more specific, some more particular, all of which function as potential

instrumental values that become actual instrumental values when the
intrinsic values become actualized.   Many things causing intrinsic
values have natures that exist and function whether or not they ever
cause intrinsic values. They may be said to have conditional potential
instrumental value. Only when all of the things necessary for the
causing of an intrinsic value cooperate does their conditional
potentiality transform into actual potentiality. Some things causing
intrinsic values have natures that interdepend with the recurrent
existings of intrinsic values in such a way that their well-being benefits.

   Difficulties involved in understanding the temporary nature of
intrinsic values, the distinctions between actual and potential values,
and how intrinsic values are caused, are additional sources of popular
confusions about values.

4. Subjective and Objective Values

Are values objective or subjective, or both? Answers to this question
depend on what is meant by "subjective" and "objective." Since both
terms have many meanings, I shall limit the meanings intended here.

A. Objective.

To be objective is to be an object of attention. Analyses of experience
normally distinguish a subject as that which attends and an object as
that which is attended to. In such an analysis, subject and object are
correlative. An object is always an object for a subject, and a subject
is always aware of an object. The next section, "Apparent and Real
Values," will consider problems of separating objects from subjects
and subjects from objects, demonstrating that there is more to things
functioning as objects than their objectivity and that there is more to
selves functioning as subjects than their subjectivity.

   i. *Are intrinsic values objective?* All intrinsic values that are objects
of attention are inherently and automatically objective.   Are any
intrinsic values not objective? It seems that, at times, a person may
lapse into unattentive awareness while yet enjoying vague feelings; if
so, then a person may be enjoying intrinsic values that are not
objective in the sense that they are not the objects of direct attention.
But if such unattentive awareness still involves a vague object, rather
than no object, then the intrinsic value still involves objectivity.

Vagueness of objectivity does not eliminate objectivity completely.

ii. *Are instrumental values objective*? That is , are instrumental values objects of attention? Some are. Whenever we attempt to influence or direct the course of our experiences, the objects we use are instrumental. Such instrumental values are obviously objective. But some are not. Many more causes of our experiences exist than are known or even knowable. Only a few such causes, such instrumental values, can become objects of attention at any time. Only a few can be actually objective. Many more can be potentially objective. But most can never become objects of attention, except as included in generalizations about "all unknowable things."

B. Subjective.

i. *Are intrinsic values subjective*? That is, are intrinsic values located in subjects that attend? To the extent that feelings are attended to, or are parts of objects attended to, they are objective, and as objective they are not subjective. But to the extent that a subject owns its feelings, or locates its feelings as parts of itself, such feelings, and such intrinsic values, function subjectively. "I am enjoying this sweet flavor." "I feel contented." "I hurt." When feelings of enjoyment and suffering are identified with a subject, they are subjective. Thus, some intrinsic values, at least, are subjective in this sense. Although I may identify myself with a felt pain, I may also oppose myself to a feared object. Such object then seems completely objective; yet my feelings of fear are my own as subject, so a critical observer must doubt that what seems completely objective to a subject is always actually so.

ii. *Are instrumental values subjective*? Most are not. Yet to the extent that a self functioning as subject intends to cause effects and actually does cause effects, it functions as an instrumental value. When a subject identifies itself as a causer, it identifies itself with its own instrumentality, or instrumental values. In this sense, its instrumental values are subjective.

C. Both.

i. *Some intrinsic values are both subjective and objective at the same time*. When I comb my hair, wash my face, exercise my body, I observe what I am doing and to identify my doing it with myself as subject. When such activities are enjoyed or suffered, intrinsic goods and evils are experienced as both subjective and objective. For easily available evidence, observe anyone who is proud. Experiences differ considerably regarding whether intrinsic values are primarily objective or primarily subjective. When enjoying a beautiful sunset, a person experiences the intrinsic value as primarily objective. When having a tantrum or a fit of anger, the feelings are experienced as primarily subjective. Certainly many intrinsic values are both.

ii. *Some instrumental values are both subjective and objective at the same time.* When combing your hair, you may enjoy the sensations involved and then comb some more in the same way to cause recurrent enjoyment. Identifying self as subject causing enjoyment is functioning as instrumental, and responding to the observed enjoyment by combing again constitutes the observed enjoyment of functioning as instrumental value also. But most instrumental values are neither subjective nor objective because they exist beyond experience.

Difficulties involved in distinguishing and keeping the distinctions clear between subjective and objective values in the senses discussed here, and between subjective and objective intrinsic values and subjective and objective instrumental values, to say nothing of other meanings of subjective and objective, are additional sources of confusion regarding values.

5. Apparent and Real Values

All objects are apparent in that they appear in awareness. Apparent objects, for present purposes, are of two main kinds, (1) those that are given and accepted as appearances and (2) those that appear to be real or to be such that they exist when not in awareness or when not apparent.

Apparently real objects may appear (1) to be partly apparent and partly real (there appears to be more to the object than appears), (2) to exist as real (when not apparent) in the same way that it appears, and (3) to exist as real in a way that is different from the way it appears. Exploration of apparently real objects is reserved for the next chapter, "How Values Are Known." Axiology as a science of values remains inadequate as long as the epistemology, the science of knowledge, used by the axiologist remains inadequate. An adequate theory of values involves an adequate theory about apparently real values and about real values, if any.

A. Intrinsic Values.

i. *Are all intrinsic values apparent*? Yes. All occur in awareness and as such are apparent. For a feeling of enjoyment or suffering to occur is to appear in awareness. Without appearance no intrinsic value exists actually.

ii. *Are all intrinsic values apparently real*? No. Some enjoyed objects are enjoyed contemplatively, that is, merely as appearances.

iii. *Are some intrinsic values apparently real*? Yes. The sweetness I am enjoying appears to me to be located in the candy bar. The beauty of the work of art I am admiring appears to me to be in the work of art. The goal I am seeking is desired because it appears to me to be or to have an intrinsic value worthy of my striving. Some intrinsic values appear to me to be real, or to exist in objects that also exist as more than what appears.

iv. *Are some intrinsic values real*? Some intrinsic values exist as real. Other persons are real and their enjoyments and sufferings are real, not in the sense that they exist outside of those persons, but in the sense that they exist outside of me as a knower of them. I judge that those apparent intrinsic values do really exist in those persons. That is, they are real in that they exist in those persons whether or not I know about them. They are real relative to me and my experiences.

v. *Are some intrinsic values pragmatically real*? Among those apparently real objects and values entertained with some uncertainty, an "as if real" quality of the apparent reality is accepted tentatively and tried out in relevant contexts. Someone advises me that I will enjoy eating at a new restaurant. In accepting the advice I enjoyably project an enjoyable ideal. The ideal might not be justified in fulfillment. But the tentatively attributed reality to the idealized intrinsic value has a kind of practical reality that causes (functions as an instrumental value) me to go to the new restaurant and dine. This kind of appearing tentatively as if real should not be underestimated in understanding value experiences, just as the working hypotheses (also tentative proposals about what appears that may work in solving problems) should not be underestimated in understanding science. A kind of facticity about those fictions leads us eventually to desired goals. That such facticity should be exploited naturally in value ventures is to be expected.

I have neglected to examine ideas about self, such as apparent self and real self and the apparent and apparently real intrinsic values of self. Self is sometimes identified with apparent intrinsic value (as when I enjoy feeling proud of myself). Self is sometimes conceived as having or being real intrinsic value (as whenever I believe that there is more to my self and its intrinsic value than appears to me at any one time). The multitudes of ways in which a self may conceive itself and to incorporate ideas of intrinsic value into such conceptions seems endless. The pragmatic realism regarding ideas of a self's intrinsic and instrumental values should not be underestimated. Self and its values are of sufficient importance that a distinct science of self is warranted. Such a science could, and should, be included among the value sciences.

B. Instrumental Values.

i. *Are all instrumental values apparently real?* No. Some merely apparent values appear to influence other merely apparent values. When my eyes are closed, sometimes I observe a flux of beautiful colors and patterns such that later movements appear to be influenced by earlier movements.

ii. *Are some instrumental values apparently real?* Yes. The candy bar inferred to be the locus of intrinsic value is also inferred to be an instrumental value not depending on its appearance for its existence. I found it already existing in a box, and left half of it on my desk for several days.

iii. *Are some instrumental values real?* Yes. Most instrumental values are real, that is, exist whether known or not.

iv. *Are some instrumental values pragmatically real?* Yes. Most of our ideas about things and their uses are pragmatic ventures. Those ventures habitually succeeding generate confidence and even dogmatic convictions about them. So most apparent instrumental values retain a pragmatic reality about them.

Difficulties in keeping clear distinctions between apparent and real values, including apparent and apparently real intrinsic values, and the varieties and variations in pragmatically real conceptions of intrinsic values, of things and of selves, are sources of popular and professional confusion about values.

6. Pure and Mixed Values

Although intrinsic values doubtless are experienced in relatively pure form (as when you stub your toe in the dark), most intrinsic values are experienced as mixed and blended in many different ways. The four distinguishable kinds of goods and bads (feelings of pleasantness and unpleasantness, of desirousness and apathy, of satisfaction and frustration, and of contentment and disturbance) are mixed and blended in different ways at different times, and their co-mingling in experience with many varieties of instrumental values (as actual values with potential values, as subjective values with objects, and as apparent values with apparently real values) presents an investigator with a plethora of mixtures.

Complicated as these are, more complications must be observed when feelings of enjoyment and suffering are combined with percepts, concepts, and with the products of creative imagination. A person needs a catalogue of human knowledge (such as the Library of Congress system of classification) to begin to classify the values occurring as mixtures with ideas and objectives. Many accounts of the kinds of values essential to human existence have been published. I resist preparing a classifactory list here. Many of the problems that people have regarding values stem from other kinds of factors with which the values are mixed. The roles of culturally inherited problems regarding ideas of values is also widely recognized. The primary task of the axiologist is to understand values in general, especially intrinsic and instrumental values. But the task is not fully completed until all of the different kinds of values (ways in which values are mixed with other factors in experience) retain their nature as values in and through all such experiences have been examined. So interpreted, axiology is, like many other sciences, a permanent project.

We shall mention more kinds of mixtures in chapter Five, "Other Value Sciences."

Difficulties resulting from mixing and blending intrinsic and instrumental values with many varieties and varying conceptions of things are also sources of confusion regarding the nature of values.

More Value Distinctions

My experience as a teacher of value theory has taught me that the
following additional distinctions are needed to clarify the language
commonly employed in trying to understand the nature of values.

A. A "Thing" and Its "Value."

Difficulties in understanding values sometimes occur relative to the
distinction between a thing and its value. Some things have many
values. My table is useful not only for writing on it but also for
holding books, for holding a lamp that lights my reading, and for
storing my stapler, scales, envelopes, and stamps. It could have one of
these values without having the others. I could sell it, and it could
then have different values for another person. It has many conditional
potential values.

B. "Having Value" and "Being Value."

But some things *are* values. After distinguishing between a thing and
its value, we are faced with the question of distinguishing between a
thing having a value and a thing being a value. A feeling of enjoyment
is a thing. It is an intrinsic value. If and when it motivates behavior
resulting in recurrence of the feeling of enjoyment, it is also an
instrumental value. An intrinsic value exists. It is a value. A person
who has a feeling of enjoyment is a thing that has such value. Yet,
such enjoyment is a part of this person. It is a part of this person's
being. To the extent that this person's being includes intrinsic values
as parts, this person is that intrinsic value.

The problem being raised here is partly a problem in axiology and
partly in metaphysics and language. Whether a thing *is* its parts,
because it includes them, or whether a thing *has* its parts, because each
part can be distinguished as owned by the thing, continues to be a
problem inherent in our metaphysics and our language generally, and
is not something peculiar to understanding values. I do not suggest
some standardized clarification of the issues here (Bahm, 1974b, chs.
6, 9, 10, 15). They are inherent in our ways of thinking and speaking
about things. Since these same problems recur in trying to understand
values, attention to the problem and to the kinds of distinctions to be

kept clear is warranted.

For example, we may distinguish between:

i. *A thing and its intrinsic value*: (1) A thing and the intrinsic value that it has. (2) A thing and the intrinsic value that it is.

ii. *A thing and its instrumental value*: (1) A thing and the instrumental value that it has. (2) A thing and the instrumental value that it is.

iii. *A thing involving both intrinsic and instrumental value*: (1) A thing and the intrinsic value that it has and the instrumental value that it has. (2) A thing and the intrinsic value that it is and the instrumental value that it is. (3) A thing and the intrinsic value that it has and the instrumental value that it is. (4) A thing and the intrinsic value that it is and the instrumental value that it has.

Whenever clarity regarding these distinctions becomes essential to understanding a problem of value, failure to be aware of and to keep clear these distinctions contributes to confusion, popular and professional.

C. "Values" and "Value Judgments".

Values, both intrinsic and instrumental, may exist whether or not judgments are made about them. A person may enjoy a sweet sensation without formulating a statement about such enjoyment. A person may be aware that a candy bar is instrumental in causing the enjoyed sensation without formulating a statement about such value.

But we also often do make judgments about values. Two common kinds of value judgments need distinguishing: valuative and evaluative.

i. *Valuative judgments*. "That is good." "I like that." "This shawl is beautiful." "This bed is comfortable." "The location is desirable."

ii. *Evaluative judgments*. "This is better than that." "That is much worse than this." "This picture is more beautiful than that one." "I like this house better than that one."

Valuative judgments express beliefs about the existence of values. Evaluative judgments express beliefs about comparisons of values that exist.

Popular confusions about values and value judgments (value judgments are themselves often called "values") may be reduced if the distinction between valuative and evaluative judgments is kept in mind. Keeping such a distinction in mind is difficult because, in practical experience, the enjoying of values, and both valuative and evaluative judgments, intermingle and flow together in lively occasions.

D. "Value Judgments" and "Standards for Judging."

A particular value judgment (valuative or evaluative) may spring forth on any occasion when a person is enjoying or suffering intrinsic value or observing causal relations. When a person has made a particular kind of value judgment several times, its recurrence may endow it with a standardized character. When several persons make similar value judgments many times, their common recurrence may endow them with a socially standardized character and develop into a cultural trait. In cold weather, people commonly prefer warm clothing, and in hot weather, people commonly prefer cool clothing. Once a judgment acquires social establishment, it functions as a prejudgment about values. Since, popularly, standards for judging are spoken of as "values," understanding values will be improved if distinctions between values, value judgments, and standards for judging values can be kept in mind.

E. Other Distinctions.

Still other confusions regarding values occur because values (intrinsic and instrumental) are confused with oughts, obligations, duties, rights, habits of choosing, principles for choosing, habits of conduct, standards for behavior, mores, rules for etiquette, and laws. Distinctions needed to clarify these confusions will not be considered here. They pertain to distinctions involved in other value sciences. Some will be mentioned in Chapter Five. But fuller treatment of them is reserved for my *Ethics: The Science of Oughtness*.

Four

KNOWLEDGE OF VALUES

How are values known? In the same way that other things are known. How, then, are other things known? What is knowledge?

This question constitutes the central problem of another science, epistemology. Epistemology is a most general science in that its task is to inquire into the nature of knowledge, that is, of all kinds of knowledge. All kinds includes knowledge of values, and knowledge of oughtness and rightness, as well as scientific, business, literary, artistic, religious, and ordinary knowledge. All of these kinds of knowledge have something in common constituting them as knowledge. The first task of an epistemologist is understand knowledge in general, and then any additional characteristics of each kind of knowledge.

Axiology depends on epistemology for answers to questions about knowledge, including knowledge of values. But the epistemologist, inquiring into knowledge of values, depends on the axiologist to explain the values which are known. Removal of any deficiencies in epistemology appearing as deficiencies in axiology is a responsibility of the epistemologist primarily and of the axiologist only secondarily.

The task set for this chapter is twofold: It summarizes answers to two questions: 1. How are objects known? (What is knowledge?) 2. How are values known?   (What differences, if any, are there in knowing values as objects and knowing other kinds of objects?)

1. How Are Objects Known?

Objects are known in two ways: directly and indirectly. Thus, two basic kinds of knowledge exist: intuitive or direct knowing and inferential or indirect knowing. Intuition is immediate apprehension of what is given in awareness. Nothing intervenes between the awareness and what appears in that awareness. Inference involves a movement from something given to something else. Many kinds of inference exist, such as perceptual inferences, conceptual inferences, inductive inferences, deductive inferences, etc. All inferences involve relations. Inference involves intuitions, but a person may intuit without inferring.

Let us examine the nature and kinds of (1) intuition and (2) inference.

A. Intuition

What is intuition? Intuition is immediacy of apprehension. Whenever awareness of appearance occurs, and nothing intervenes between the awareness and what appears in the awareness, that awareness intuits that appearance. Intuition is the name we give to the way awareness apprehends when awareness apprehends appearance directly. No intuition exists apart from awareness. And, as I also claim, no awareness exists without intuition.

Although intuition is by nature so simple that nothing more need be said about it, I shall attempt to state and explore five general characteristics of its nature: immediacy of apprehension, omnipresence, kinds, variability, and limits.

i. *Immediacy of apprehension.* My analysis of immediacy of apprehension yields four distinguishable factors: apprehension, immediacy, appearance, and intuiter.

(1) Apprehension. To apprehend is to grasp, not in the way that a hand grasps a ball or some marbles, but in the way that what is prehended occurs in appearance all at once. Apprehension involves unity, or a unity of unities. When several objects are intuited at once, apprehension comprehends them together. Thus, the all-at-once-ness involves their togetherness. When attention appears occupied with only one object, as when contemplating the full expanse of a blue sky, unity is apparent without togetherness, unless somehow plurality is implicit in expanse. That is, apprehension involves objective unity, whether the object itself appears unified or whether many objects are unified.

Intuition may apprehend more than one object, with or without pattern, more than one event, with or without pattern, more than one quality, more than one dimension, etc. (More below under "Kinds.") Intuition may apprehend, and thus unify, not only spatial, temporal, formal, processual, qualitative, and dimensional pluralities, but also all such unifications of pluralities in a single Gestalt. Intuition as a *unity* of unities is a simple whole, nonrelational and nondimensional. But as a unity of *unities* of pluralities, intuition not only is relational and dimensional but can be multirelational and multidimensional. In fact, since all knowledge presupposes apprehension by intuition, the capacity of intuition to apprehend must extend to include all of the complexity that can be grasped in a single act of attention (or, if mind can intuitively unify successive acts of attention, then such extended unity).[1]

(2) Immediacy. Immediacy is an additional kind of unity, that is, unity of awareness and appearance or of apprehension and what is apprehended. Not only are all of the unities of pluralities united in intuitive apprehension but also the immediacy with which such awareness apprehends their appearance is itself a kind of unity. Since we can distinguish between all such factors thus unified, we can properly assert that intuition always involves organic unity. Organic unity involves a whole of parts in which the parts retain their differences while also cooperatively participating in constituting the unity of the whole.

Immediacy is not mediacy, that is, apprehension of appearance through or by means of something else. The fact that intuition involves immediacy does not prevent an intuition, including awareness, appearance, and immediacy of apprehension, from being caused or mediated. Intuition, both its whole and parts, both its unity and its pluralities, and thus its organic unity, is caused by a multiplicity of causes each one of which, when serially caused by more distant causes upon which it depends, may be a product of the mediation of such serial causes. But, even though we do not yet know much about how an intuition emerges into existence from its complex of causes, we are able to observe, that is, to inspect, its internal nature, as well as to include generalizations about its apparent ways of functioning.

(3) Appearance. What intuition apprehends is appearance. Without appearance there is no intuition. Without intuition there is no appearance. Appearance is a kind of being, even if quite temporary. Intuition immediately apprehends the being of the appearance. Thus, intuition exists, both as an act of apprehending and as apprehending the being of the appearance intuited.

What appears is sometimes called a "datum." A datum is something "given." We can have many kinds of data. British Empiricist epistemology speaks of "sense data" as the original source of all knowledge. Even though this theory has had great influence on philosophies of science, critical analysis has demonstrated its inadequacy. Instead of interpreting sense data as conglomerate elements leaving impressions in the brain or mind, later theorists

recognize that most perceptual experience is already conceptualized
and gestaltified when "given." Although a datum is something given,
it is also something "taken." For the act of apprehension not only
receives what is given but takes what it receives, and the way in which
what is given is taken, when the two are united in immediacy,
influences and modifies what is given.

Questions about how much preconditionings of the mind influence
the way data are taken continue to be issues in epistemology. A mind
can apprehend only what it has a capacity for apprehending, and
conditionings of various kinds, including formal education, influence
the way in which data are apprehended. Doubtless some intuitions are
determined more definitely by causes of what is given and some more
by causes of the way of taking. But it now seems unlikely that intuition
can occur without both kinds of causes. If so, then any theory of
knowledge, and any philosophy of science, failing to take into account
both kinds of contributions to "data" is deficient. The tendency "to
see what we look for" conditions scientific investigations much more
than is claimed by those who would eliminate all subjective bias and
wishful thinking.

Although intuited data exist as something that may serve as
foundational for inferential knowledge, automatic use of such data in
inferences has led to adding to the word "data" many other meanings.
For we now speak of compilations of information as "data," and the
results of earlier investigations being used for another investigation as
"data." The generalization of the meaning of the word "data" in
these ways causes many to overlook the foundational significance of
intuited data.

Even with initial observations of data, for example, when recalling
how the sound of a tuning fork vibration appeared a moment ago,
questions that interest the observer determine upon what attention is
focused. Attention to part of a datum is an act of abstracting.
Questions arise as to how much more is contributed by the mind when
abstracting from a datum than when intuiting it originally. A cautious
scientist will try to be continually conscious of the contributions of
personal interests to the data as intuited and as abstracted. The
distinction between "preanalytical" and "postanalytical" data is useful
to keep in mind where reliability of conclusion depends on reliability
of data (Lowenberg, 1927, 5-14).

(4) Intuiter. An act of intuition involves an actor, agent, or intuiter.

Apprehension involves an apprehender. Appearance in awareness involves something that is aware. A datum involves something to which it is given. So, as a minimum, we can say that intuition involves an intuiter. Although we spoke of intuition as apprehending and taking, implying that it had some power to apprehend and take, any power to apprehend and take doubtless exists in the intuiter as agent. How much more is required in the nature of an intuiter is a question postponed for other occasions. I know of no satisfactory solution to the mind-body problem, but the sound founding of epistemology and all other sciences depend upon eventually finding one.

ii. *Omnipresence*. Intuition is a universal condition of knowing. Whatever is mediated can be known only when it comes to rest in some moment of immediacy. As long as potential information fails to reach awareness in which its appearance is intuited, it remains potential and not actual. When you infer, you do not escape intuiting but become involved in more complex intuitions, as we shall observe in discussing inference.

If intuition is a universal condition of knowing, how are we justified in speaking of it as one of two kinds of knowledge? On the one hand, we do occasionally have experiences in which attention seems wholly occupied by what appears and with contemplating it. A person may be asked to report on what appears during contemplation. When the person reports, what is reported is knowledge. Billions of dollars expended on "consciousness-expanding drugs" serve as evidence of the commonness that some people attribute to this kind of knowledge.

iii. *Kinds*. Although intuitions are alike in consisting in the immediacy with which awareness apprehends appearance, the multiplicities of kinds of appearances involve multiplicities of kinds of intuition.[2]

To begin with one kind of intuition, sensory intuition, we find many different kinds of sensory end-organs, each contributing its sensation, one of which, visual, includes sensations of pattern and color. Color includes primary colors and their shades and hues and mixtures and blends, numbering altogether in the thousands. So our "one kind of intuition, sensory," already involves thousands of kinds of intuition. Sensory patterns include millions of static forms and patterns of movement, rhythms, waves, gyrations, oscillations, spirals, and helices, as well as natural patterns.

Perceptual and conceptual intuitions are more complex, usually gestaltified, intermingled with memorial and anticipatory images, and often enmeshed in linguistic, including metaphorical, and other cultural intricacies. We abstract ideas of numbers, relations, dimensions and systems only by intuiting what is abstracted and that from which we abstract. We intuit feelings, emotions, hopes, fears, regrets, and longings. We intuit differences and likenesses, distinctions and continuities, associations and separations, vagueness and clearness, implications and inconsistencies. We intuit each of the kinds of value outlined in the previous chapter: good and bad, ends and means, actual and potential, subjective and objective, apparent and real, pure and mixed.

The significance of the many kinds of intuition becomes clearer when we examine the multitude of inferences, all of which continuously involve intuition. Treatment of inferences in the next section is an extension of the present treatment of intuition.

iv. *Variability*. Intuition varies in many ways, including ways relative to each of the four distinguished factors: apprehension, immediacy, appearance, and intuiter.

(1) Intuitions vary in magnitude, complexity, and intensity of grasp, depending on duration, as longer or shorter, of pulses of attention, on the complexity or simplicity of the contents of appearance, and on the vitality of the intuiter during an act of attention.

(2) Intuitions vary relative to immediacy. Although, on the one hand, immediacy is immediacy, which has no degrees, on the other hand, intuition is apprehension of appearance and appearances often involve apparent mediacies. Awareness of incompleteness, unfinishedness, and uncertainty evidently requiring something not given to complete, finish, and certify what is apprehended incorporates need for mediation of what is apprehended. When both mediacy and immediacy are present in intuition, the immediacy must share that intuition with such mediacy. An intuition does not cease to be constituted by its immediacy, for the apparent incompleteness or uncertainty are also apprehended immediately. An apparent mediacy must itself be immediately apprehended. But when the amounts and kinds of mediacy constitute larger portions of appearance, an intuition is constituted by larger portions of mediacy as well as by immediacy. Some intuitions, such as those primarily contemplative, involve immediacy that may be entirely free from evident mediacy. Some intuitions, such as those apprehending overwhelming fear, involve

immediacy of appearance saturated with mediacy. In this way, immediacy varies.

Immediacy is transparent, not in the sense that vision is required, but in that it does not call attention to itself when it exists. It has no influence upon either awareness or appearance, except as a condition of their mutual existence. Yet, because all of the many appearances make a difference in the kind of awareness, immediacy must be able, not to mediate, but *to immediate all* of those different kinds. Being transparent, immediacy becomes occupied by and transmits all that appears (including all appearances lacking transparency). In this way, intuition is always transparent, and thus is transparent to apparent intransparencies.

(3) Intuitions vary relative to appearances. The variety data is endless. Understanding variations in the relative contributions to appearance as given (discovered) and appearances as taken (created) is needed in attempts to assure reliable knowledge. The relative amounts of contributions from memory, anticipation, creative imagination, subconscious fears, and manias, as well as from sensory, perceptual, and conceptual sources, continue to be intriguing problems for epistemologists. Current research on varieties of brain waves should provide new insights regarding the sources of appearance.

(4) Intuition varies with intuiters. The general health, present body tonicity, relevant past experiences, habits and skills, embodiment of cultural resources, social encouragement, environmental conduciveness, and psychological readiness all affect how an intuiter intuits. Intuition as transparent immediacy of apprehension has no power. But the vitality with which the intuiter intuits provides whatever power is needed for intuiting. Persons vary from moment to moment, from hour to hour, from day to day, from month to month, and at different stages in life, from infancy to old age. Persons vary in alertness not only due to vitality but also due to presented dangers. And persons differ mentally, but the nature of mind is still sufficiently mysterious that statements about its contributions to variations in intuition should await further research.

v. *Limits.* Limits exist relative to each of the characteristics of intuition. Scientists who are acquainted with the limitations of knowledge involved in the speeds of light, sound, X-rays, radio waves, etc., often remain unaware of the limitations on knowledge inherent in intuition and its characteristics and conditions of existence and functioning. Some efforts to expand present limits may be successful. Although "consciousness-expanding drugs" have brought some temporary neural invigoration and some more clarified alertness, thus far no great advance in human knowledge has resulted, as far as I know. The normal way to transcend the limits of intuition is through inference, to which we turn next.

B. Inference.

Inference is going from something given to something else, or from one appearance to another appearance. The "going" is mental and involves awareness, although some inferences also involve overt body action. Inferences are of many kinds.

Some inferences occurring within one act of attention are completed within that act, and so are intuited. For example, although a young child learning to count may find apprehending the inference, "2 + 2 = 4," quite difficult, a person skilled in arithmetic can intuit the inference, as speed tests have made evident. Inferences completed in one act of attention are intuited.

Some inferences occurring in one act of attention involve an appearance of incompleteness. Each of the many kinds of inference has its apparent kind of incompleteness. I select for consideration perceptual inference, conceptual inference, inductive inference, deductive inference, and complex inference.

i. *Perceptual inference.* Perception involves sensation. I select from the many kinds of perception an example from visual perception. When I look at a table, only part of its surface, that on the side which I am viewing, appears in my vision. Because I am familiar with this table, I infer that it has another side not appearing in my vision. Such inference may be said to be going from what is given to what is not given. The surface on my side of the table is given; the surface on the other side is not given. My perception of the table involves the inference that it has another side that is not visible. But, although the visibility of the other side is not given, the nonvisibility of the other side is given, or at least it is given inferentially when I attend to it. Or, also although the appearance of the other side is not given, appearance of its lack of visual appearance is given. Such perceptual inference is a going from what is given to what is not given by way of going from what is given to what is *given* as not given. Both of these givens are intuited together in the inference.

My perceptions of tables in pictures and movies often involve the same kinds of inferences as of real tables. That is, I normally perceive tables in pictures and movies as well as real tables as having another side that is not visible. Does perceiving a real table (an apparently real table the appearance of which is caused by a real table) require an additional inference regarding its reality? Answers to this question will depend on how critical the perceiver is about perception.

As naive realists, uncritical of our perceptual inferences, no additional inference is intended. When what appears as if real is given, its apparent reality is accepted as given. Although an inference that what appears as real exists whether apparent or not is implicit in accepting as given the appearance as real, as naive realists we habitually apprehend our perceptions (and implicit inferences) of apparently real things unquestioningly.

Some perceptions occur in single pulses of awareness. But in some naively realistic perceptions, tables appear as enduring beyond a single pulse and even seem to have an independent substantiality expected to last indefinitely. Problems of how apparent tables persist in mind through a series of awarenesses still baffle epistemologists. But when apparent tables do so persist, perceptual inferences transcend single pulses of attention and inductive processes inherent in mind-brain functioning work automatically. Prolonged perception of a single object already involves inductive cumulation even without a person being aware that inductive processes are involved.

ii. *Conceptual inference*. Perception involves both sensation and conception. So we have already involved conceptual inference in our example about an apparent table. But we also abstract concepts and treat them as if they were independent entities. Having observed several tables with rectangular tops, a person may abstract the concept of rectangularity. If we have defined the concept clearly, we can deduce that it has two pairs of sides having equal lengths. Given the concept of rectangularity as a whole, we can go from such a whole to observing its parts as given. We may be aware of the whole without attending to its parts, so an act of inferring that the whole has certain parts is a distinguishable act of attention. When the inference has been completed, intuition of the concept, intuition of the parts of the concept, and intuition that the concept as a whole has such parts, have all appeared in awareness. Some conceptual inferences occur in a single pulse of awareness, others require several pulses and some still longer times.

People tend to be naive realists about their concepts. Although critical reflection should reveal the experiential origins of concepts and that abstracting omits much in the experiences from which concepts have been abstracted, uncritical thinking ignores what has been omitted when attention is focused on what has been abstracted. People are naturally naively realistic about abstracted concepts unless they have been alerted by the problem of error. This tendency to regard concepts as real is called "reification."

Endowing concepts with reality entails endowing their implications with reality. When concepts are interpreted as real essences, or essentials, implications of such concepts are regarded as necessary, or as necessities.[3] Hence persons succumbing to these natural tendencies also become insistent about accepting deduced conclusions and adopting dogmatic attitudes regarding them.

Just as we should be critical about naive realism regarding the reality of perceived objects appearing as if real, so we should be critical about the reality of conceptual objects appearing as if real. Let us turn now to such criticisms.

(1) Naive realism is untenable. It has no solution to the problem of error. Awareness of error occurs when what appears to be so also appears to be not so. A rod half submerged in water appears both bent or broken to visual perception yet unbent and unbroken to tactile perception and to visual perception when it is withdrawn from the water.[4] As naive realists, we are committed to accepting appearances of reality just as they appear. When two appearances contradict, the contradiction appears. In practice as naive realists, we may accept one or the other of two contradictory appearances as true and reject the other as false or illusory. But we have no explanation for the appearance of perceptual error.

(2) Inquiries into the causes of contradiction bring us now to a view that has been called "Scientific Realism." This is the view of the nature of knowledge that we would hold when utilizing all recently known scientific conclusions about knowing in formulating it. For example, our apparently real table appears constructed of solid wood. But chemists explain that wood consists of cells, consisting of molecules, consisting of atoms, consisting of subatomic particles gyrating dynamically with areas of space between them, so that the

seemingly solid table is really mostly space and tiny particles gyrating regularly to keep the surface fairly stable and seemingly solid. Visual perception involves a light source, light rays reflecting from the table surface and travelling through the atmosphere, lenses and liquids in the eye, transformation of light rays into nervous impulses in rods and cones in the retina, passage of such impulses to two halves of the cortex, and finally, though not understood, to the production of an apparent table. Even after causal processes have been explained completely, questions remain about how we can be sure that attention to an apparent table involves a genuine reference to the real table that is believed to be so unlike the apparent table.

Acceptance of Scientific Realism clearly rejects naive realism. However, Scientific Realism itself is based on conclusions by scientists and upon the experiences of those scientists operating much of the time as naive realists. That is, the conclusions of scientists used in formulating Scientific Realism are not self-evident. They have to be demonstrated. Many of the same criticisms raised against naive realism hold against Scientific Realism. Furthermore, as scientific investigations advance, some conclusions on which Scientific Realism was based when first formulated are no longer justified. Some Scientific Realists who are also conceptual realists have been dogmatic about their epistemological conclusions. Not only has their dogmatism proved unjustified in some cases, but awareness of the need for tentativity regarding hypotheses held as conclusions should make epistemologists aware than any theory of knowledge claiming scientific adequacy must retain an attitude of tentativity. Since any scientific conclusions used in formulating Scientific Realism as a theory of knowledge should be held with an attitude of tentativity, so should Scientific Realism as an hypotheses be held with an attitude of tentativity.

(3) Tentativity as a condition of the scientific attitude and method leads us to "Pragmatic Realism." By "Pragmatic Realism" I mean that theory of knowledge that keeps tentativity regarding hypotheses and conclusions ever-present while search continues for more and more understanding of things and of knowledge. Whereas the Scientific Realism of an earlier day crystallized its theory of knowledge in terms of conclusions crystallized from various sciences, Pragmatic Realism continues to be conscious of the incompleteness of scientific discoveries, including many concerning knowledge, mind, awareness,

appearance, intuition, and inference.

Realistic hypotheses, both those of naive realism and those of earlier Scientific Realism, worked, and still work, to some extent. But so do idealistic and antiscientific hypotheses. Pragmatic Realism is committed to giving all working hypotheses a hearing and to examining whatever is presented as evidence. Unfortunately, as long as scientists are willing to conduct investigations and assert conclusions in terms of a particular theory of knowledge at a time when such theories prevail, they may claim to be pragmatic but they are not justified in claiming certainty. Deciding which among prevailing theories of knowledge is most nearly adequate is itself a scientific problem, and one that is much neglected. I propose that we continue to operate as Pragmatic Realists at least until we have obtained more understanding of the mind-brain interdependencies and have deliberately tested alternative theories of knowledge. If and when we do achieve reliable consensus after such research and testing, another name for the most adequate epistemology may well emerge.

Conceptual inferences occur in minds. When concepts appear to have implications, a person naturally accepts inferences revealing or recognizing those implications as necessary. But does such necessity have any reality? A person may draw the same conclusions repeatedly and accumulate evidence of reliability. The concept of rectangularity always implies two pairs of sides having equal lengths. But the assumption that concepts, such as rectangularity, have a reality independent of minds, although it does have a Pragmatic Realistic warrant for those who work with it, strikes me as unnecessary and misleading. The problems of getting supposedly real conceptual forms from wherever they are into minds just in time for each act of conception are insurmountable and presuppose more mysticism and magic than can be justified by any scientific demonstration. Problems of communicating concepts from one mind to another through well-known channels of communication are sufficiently difficult without adding insurmountable difficulties.

One way in which concepts do exist really is that concepts exist in the minds of others whether I know them or not. Such concepts, although not real in existing independently of minds, are real in existing independently of some minds when existing in other minds. Furthermore, socialized communication has produced socialized thinking, aided by language, printing, libraries, and educational systems. Conceptual mores have a social reality. They exist as commonly accepted beliefs, and children or other inductees into a society learn that they already exist, that is, really exist, in the prevailing culture. But, even though social realities often have great stability, they are also subject to change. Schools of scientists, subscribing to one philosophy of science and to many scientific conclusions, sometimes experience periods of enduring stability only to have them revised in light of new evidence.

The social reality of concepts enables people to cooperate with greater facility and reliability. But continuing attitude of tentativity regarding even their social reality is advisable, not merely as a general scientific principle but also because our understanding of communications between minds still leaves much to be desired. The social reality of concepts is the warrant for requiring that scientific experiments be repeatable by other scientists. Conceptual inferences can be tested by appeal to others to the extent that others can conceive the same concepts. Science is a social enterprise.

iii. *Inductive inference.* Induction involves intuition of each particular appearance and of one or more particular likenesses given in two or more particular appearances. A statement about such likenesses is a generalization. Induction involves a mind as an agency transcending particular appearances, aware of similarities and differences, able to remember previous appearances, and able to generalize. When all objects of a particular kind have been observed, induction is said to be complete. But when not all objects of a kind have been observed, induction remains incomplete.

The more numerous the objects and the more complex the objects under investigation, the more likely induction will be incomplete. When objects being observed are numerous, or involve numerous likenesses or traits being examined, investigators naturally employ numbers and whatever measurements and calculations seem appropriate. Measurements depend on instruments, so questions about the suitability of instruments, their reliability, acceptable units of measurement, degrees of precision possible or probable, availability for use, etc., are relevant to understanding induction. Theory of probability, including probable error, and how to settle conflicts when different investigators reach different conclusions, are normal concerns of inductive scientists.

When several generalizations support each other, constituting an explanatory system, the mores of scientists require that a new inductive generalization be examined also regarding its consistency with the system. When it does, such consistency may be regarded as additional evidence of the reliability of the system. When it does not, it is suspect and the adequacy of the system is challenged until the apparent inconsistency is explained or either it or the system is modified. Long-range difficulties occur when different sciences, each having its problems, methods of induction, and system of conclusions, strengthen systemic consistency within their fields but neglect testing for consistency with systems in other fields. Systemic induction remains incomplete until consistency has been achieved with all other fields, including the more general fields of metaphysics and axiology, and with that comprehensive philosophy resulting from combining the systemic conclusions of the various sciences into a cohesive whole (Bahm, 1980, 29-35).

iv. *Deductive inference*. Although deduction is often already present in simple perceptual and conceptual inferences, I focus here on logical theory and abstract systems. Although the history of logics is long and complicated, symbolic logics, like that expounded in *Principia Mathematica* (Whitehead, 1910), now prevail in many scientific circles. Logicians idealizing perfect precision available only by premising excluded middles between atomic terms, classes, and propositions so that they have nothing in common, postulate sets (the fewer the better) and formal rules of operation, have devised symbolic systems expressing perfectly clear distinctions. Difficulties with such systems include irrelevancy to existence as experienced and replacement of implication with "material implication," a relation sterilized of all implicitness.

Symbolic logic becomes a game. Correlations between its extremely abstract structures and concrete existence are few. Applications of the logic require additional postulates about how relevant the logic is to practical problems, and these postulates often involve additional implicative logic that is largely neglected while symbolic logicians emphasize their gaming. Science exists more fully in engineering and other applied sciences because in them explanatory theory receives a testing of abstract and practical postulates usually not available for completely abstract systems. Hasty misapplication of symbolic logic by enthusiastic digital computer programmers has resulted in costly malpractice mistakenly threatening the confidence of research managers in computer reliability (Bahm, 1969, 175-177).

Deductive inferences are mental acts. For example, "if A is larger than B, and B is larger than C, then A is larger than C." Such an inference involves a series of intuitions. A person intuits A, intuits B, intuits the relationship "larger than" and its holding between A and B, intuits the proposition, "A is larger than B," intuits C, intuits B and that B is the same B previously intuited, and intuits the relation "larger than" and its holding between B and C, intuits the proposition "B is larger than C," intuits as a self-evident principle that "if A is larger than B, and B is larger than C, then A is larger than C," and intuits that the inference is true. Even such a simple inference involves a series of intuitions.

We do not escape intuition by becoming involved in more complex inferences, but engage in more, and more complex, intuitions. Persons becoming familiar with regular forms of deduction learn to rely on previous intuitions and to skip some steps in deductive demonstrations. Deducers often develop reliable habits of deduction just as walkers develop reliable habits of walking. As long as our habits are reliable, we may meet similar situations with fewer actual intuitions, but this involves a synthesizing function of the mind still not well understood.

v. *Complex inferences.* Distinguishing between perceptual and conceptual and between inductive and deductive inferences (I have neglected many other kinds, such as memorial inferences, anticipatory inferences, imaginative inferences) may be helpful in understanding inferential knowledge. Yet, in practice all of these kinds intermingle so constantly and so intimately that abstracting each as a distinct kind may be misleading. Scientific methods used in dealing with problems normally employ all kinds, and questions about the relative importance of inductive and deductive methods for science have been vigorously debated.

The roles of systems in understanding how objects are known tend to be neglected. If we have achieved sufficient understanding of two or more systems, we tend to keep them clear in our thinking. But when we are immersed in multilingual, multicultural, multiscience, and multisectarian influences without achieving comprehension of any one of them, our interpretations of objects often reveal inconsistencies inherent in conflicts between the systems of ideas dominating each such influence. Knowledge of objects is conditioned by complexes of influences, many of them systems of interpretation personally acquired or culturally inherited.

Difficulties in understanding the nature of inferences, the omnipresence of intuition in knowledge, the intermingling of intuition and inference, the many kinds of inferences and their intermingling, and the roles of systems and systemic conflicts in influencing interpretations, all contribute to confusions, popular and professional, about values. Difficulties in understanding knowledge function as difficulties in understanding values.

2. How Are Values Known?

Values are known in the same ways that other objects are known, that is, by intuition and inference. Anyone who understands knowledge already understands knowledge of values. Different kinds of values, each involving its way of knowing, do exist, just as different kinds of other objects (electrons, peaches, cyclones, X-rays) exist, each involving its way of knowing. Our concern here, as in the first part of this chapter, is limited to some general similarities.

A. Intuition.

How do we know values, both intrinsic and instrumental, by means of intuition?

i. *Intrinsic values.* Intrinsic values are known intuitively, at least in their pure forms. When you are enjoying a sweet flavor, a feeling of enthusiasm, a feeling of satisfaction, or a feeling of contentment, your enjoyment is self-evident. No uncertainty regarding the end-in-itself quality of your enjoyment is present, unless conceptual factors intrude to contribute doubt or distortion to a complex experience. Initially, that is, in their pure forms, intrinsic values are known with as much certainty as any other intuited objects. Conceptual factors also intrude into some intuitions of colors, distances, durations, and numbers to contribute doubt or distortion to how they are intuited. Difficulties in observing intrinsic values as data for scientific investigation are similar to difficulties in observing other kinds of data when they are mixed and intermingled in complex Gestalts sometimes gyrating kaleidoscopically. But deliberate efforts to isolate and abstract intrinsic values as data can provide information as reliable regarding intrinsic values as regarding other kinds of intuited objects.

A problem some people have in reporting value experiences has to do with adequate linguistic ability. Elementary education usually requires acquiring ability in arithmetic and general science, but, except in those schools emphasizing theory and practice in the arts, achievement of ability to discriminate the multiplicities of kinds of value distinctions is not generally required. Sensory pleasures are of many sorts, and colors alone have endless varieties as single colors, to say nothing of additional varieties of combinations. The *Munsell Manual of Color* (Cooper, 1941) distinguishes five major hues (red, yellow, green, blue, purple), nine degrees of intensity (on a white-black range), and from four to ten degrees of chroma, for each color. Its page illustrating red colors presents forty-one varieties. Persons able to distinguish all of these varieties, or even pink from scarlet and maroon, have a better vocabulary for describing their color experiences and feelings associated with them as better incentives for adding to distinctions between tints and shades that are missed by persons who can distinguish between only the five major hues.

As long as educational provisions and requirements neglect learning about intrinsic values, whether sensory pleasures and pains, feelings of desirousness and apathy, satisfaction and frustration, or contentment and disturbance, we can expect a deficiency in appreciation and in vocabulary suited for expressing more varieties and subtle discriminations and ranges of variations of intrinsic values. Although intuition is automatic, even instinctive, what is intuited is a matter of personal experience and training. To the extent that knowledge of intrinsic values depends upon such experience, training, and vocabulary, any scientific investigation by axiologists will be facilitated or handicapped accordingly. Similar problems faced by physical scientists regarding the training needed for reliable intuiting and reporting of data needed in investigations are well known. When axiologists receive as many years of technical training as research physicists, the technical knowledge of intrinsic values needed as bases for the other value sciences may be expected to be of equal abstractness, intricacy, and reliability.

ii. *Instrumental values.* Some instrumental values are intuited. For example, enjoyment of the sweetness resulting from eating a candy bar causes me to desire more, to use my muscles, hand, fingers, lips, etc., to place the bar in my mouth, where I bite and chew it and taste the sweetness enjoyed again. All of the apparent causes are intuited. As objects of knowledge, these instrumental values are known by intuition. Many other causes are not intuited. Many cannot be known. Many may be known inferentially.

B. Inference.

How do we know values, both intrinsic and instrumental, by means of inference?

i. *Intrinsic values*. Many intrinsic values may be known inferentially. (1) Perceptually, I infer, from perceiving my brother also eating a candy bar and seeming to enjoy its sweetness, that intrinsic value, both as sensory pleasure and feeling of satisfaction, now exists in him also. (2) Conceptually, I infer, from his statement, that slower chewing and swallowing prolongs his enjoyment of sweetness, that the intrinsic value existing in his sensory pleasure is less intense than mine. (3) Inductively, I infer from repeated enjoyments of eating a brand of candy bar that eating a candy bar of that brand always produces the same kind of intrinsic value. (4) Deductively, I infer from the premise, "Eating this brand of candy bar always produces enjoyment," that I will enjoy, or experience intrinsic value, next time when I eat one.

Complex inferences, including those inferring the existence of intrinsic values in apparently real objects, whether naively, Scientifically, or Pragmatically, will receive some comments needed to reveal the kinds of problems facing axiologists.

(1) On the one hand, naively realistic inferences that intrinsic good exists in candy bars whether known or not are epistemologically untenable. Perceived intrinsic good exists in perceived objects no more than do sweetness, color, or solidity. On the other hand, the practical personal and social workability and acceptability of naive realistic inferences about solidity, color, sweetness, and intrinsic goodness have a pragmatic justification that epistemologists, including axiologists, must take into account. The obvious as-if-real appearance of objects must be accepted at face value until challenged by apparent error. Even after such challenge, and after indoctrination by Scientific Realists, many persons still see many objects as obviously as-if-real, and as solid, colored, sweet, and intrinsically good.

The pragmatic justification for holding as practically true some views demonstrated to be false by Scientific Realists calls for explanation. But the problem is the same for naive views about numbers, and their seeming reality, necessity, and reliability. The faith of some mathematicians in the reality of numbers has a practical, pragmatic justification even though the view is false. Numbers too exist only in minds, in awareness. But the naive faith that numbers are real has a practical justification. The practical justifications of faith in the reality of numbers as well as in intrinsic values equally call for explanation. Without exploring the faiths of those who regard numbers as having intrinsic value, especially those having convictions about "lucky numbers" or "unlucky numbers," I will explain why epistemologically untenable naive realism must still be accredited as having some warrant.

Most of the justification consists in the practical usefulness of naive realistic beliefs evolved through biological struggles for existence. The emergence of minds and visual perception involved perceiving objects as dangers or as food. Their existence external to the body required perceiving them as real. The ability to perceive molecules, atoms, electrons, etc., did not develop then. But working conceptions of grosser objects, such as tigers, trees, water, berries, sky, wind, and mates, were necessary for survival. Perceived as desirable or harmful, such objects were thereby perceived as good or bad, and the goodness and badness of the objects were naturally located in the objects. A person can also observe infants forced to learn to perceive cradle, nipple, toys, and pins as real objects inherently good or bad. To reject as untenable biologically induced naive realistic beliefs about objects, as physicists and other scientists do, and as a careful epistemologist must do, is to reject some quite practical beliefs. Let us consider Scientific Realism and then return to problems of justifying practical realism.

(2) Scientific Realism has drawn on numerous sciences to describe the conditions of knowing; on physics for light waves and lenses, on chemistry for electro-chemical transformations in rods and cones, on neurology for transmission of nervous impulses, on physiological psychology for evidence about brain waves. Except for physiological accounts of the causes of emotions and neurological efforts to correlate unpleasant and pleasant feelings with variations in synaptic resistance, little effort has been devoted to accounting for the emergence of values.

Recent challenges of the view that science cannot deal with values have encouraged more scientists to investigate further. For example,

Biologist R.W. Sperry, contends that "conscious or mental phenomena are dynamic, emergent, pattern (or configurational) properties of the living brain in action," and that "these emergent properties in the brain have causal control potency" (Sperry, 1966, 3). He declares that "Human values are inherently properties of brain activity" (Sperry, 1972, 115-1130), and function causally in influencing bodily (and consequently social[5]) behavior. I am sympathetic with Sperry's views and efforts. Intrinsic values are caused and at least sometimes causal. Yet something about an emergent intrinsic value cannot be explained entirely in terms of brain causes. Intrinsic values, as the ultimate bases for moral appeals, have a nature and ultimacy that cannot be reduced to brain activity even though intrinsic value cannot exist apart from such activity and are constantly and directly conditioned and caused by such activity. After a mind has developed considerable substantiality, we can as truly say that the brain is a property of the mind as that the mind is a property of the brain. As a result of studying Chinese philosophy, I now regard mind and brain as mutually immanent. When a mature mind ceases to function permanently, its brain, and body, degenerate, decompose, and cease to function permanently.

(3) "Pragmatic Realism" is the name I give to those scientific realistic efforts recognizing the natural role of intrinsic values in the biological struggle for existence (including "ontology recapitulates phylogeny"). Pragmatic Realism recognizes the role of intrinsic values in the motivations of scientists to achieve greater understanding of the purpose of improving and enjoying life. That a real world exists is taken for granted. But the nature of that world continues to be problematic for human survival and enjoyment, even though many uniformities have been discovered and many solutions to problems work very reliably. Although the universal prevalence among people of the four kinds of intrinsic value is one of those uniformities, beliefs about those values and how they are caused, recur, are maintained, and are terminated emerge variously in different persons and cultures. Despite cultural encrustation of some such beliefs, for centuries and even millennia, each continues to exist as a pragmatic venture to which one or more persons is more or less committed. Some beliefs become personal habits. Some become social mores. But many function as ideals, or as ideas of goods to be realized. And these ideals appear to have an objective reality. To the extent that they motivate us to achieve them, they have a practical reality, a pragmatic reality, which

must be recognized as an object of knowledge.

The presence of false elements in many culturally established ideals influence knowledge in physics as well as in axiology because such influences are inherent in the nature of knowing. The ideals of scientists committed to solving a problem are ideas of things that do not yet exist, though they function causally in motivating and guiding the work done in pursuing a solution. Ideas of atoms, electrons, and quarks are still ideals, for commitment to tentativity regarding even the firmest conclusions implies an element of uncertainty implicitly idealizing diminution or removal of such uncertainty. A difficulty in knowing values as objects is inherent in knowing objects. When knowledge is conceived as pragmatic venturing, theories about values, both values in general and particular values, are more likely to receive recognition as scientifically justifiable equally with theories about other kinds of things.

ii. *Instrumental values.* Discussion of inferences about instrumental values is unnecessary at this point. They are exemplified by judgments about causality in all of the sciences and technologies. The instrumental value of intrinsic values has already been discussed. When projected as ideals, they become goals causing behavior conducive to their realization.

In closing this chapter, I remind the reader that its task was to inquire into knowledge by examining two common ways of knowing objects and then to show how values are known by these same ways. Problems commonly involved in knowing objects recur as problems in knowing values, just as they recur in knowing atoms, cells, and galaxies. Knowing values as objects involves some problems peculiar to values, just as knowing about atoms, cells, and galaxies involves problems peculiar to their natures. Nothing in the nature of values prevents them from being investigated by scientific methods.

Five

OTHER VALUE SCIENCES

Axiology is the most general value science. Its primary task is to inquire into the nature of values, that is, of all values, and thus of what all values have in common. In Chapter Three, ten kinds of distinctions needed for understanding values were examined. Understanding the values studied in all of the other, less general, value sciences presupposes understanding these ten distinctions. They depend on these distinctions for providing foundational generalizations about values. But each value science supplements axiology by exploring a specific kind of value or specific ways in which values are used in dealing with other problems. Thus axiology, as a most general science, depends on each of the other value sciences for their investigations of specific kinds of values.

All of the value sciences interdepend, since discoveries made in any one of them may have implications for all of the others. Consistency of conclusions in different sciences is regarded as necessary for scientific truth. So the work of an axiologist remains incomplete as long as any of the other value sciences remain incomplete. When new kinds of values emerge, new sciences of values may emerge, and new problems of consistency may occur. Axiology has an open future. Since benefits from using scientific methods are desirable, even urgently needed, efforts to achieve reliable knowledge in all of the value sciences should be encouraged.

Although all other sciences are value sciences in that they involve values, some sciences make values their primary objects of concern. Five such sciences, or groups of sciences, have been selected for brief examination here. They are: aesthetics, ethics, religiology, economics, and policy sciences. Many others, because values are involved in their subject matters, might have been included, for example, physiology, psychology, sociology, political science, anthropology, history, human geography, and education. All of the applied and technical sciences involve values, some more consciously than others, for example, ecology, architecture, medicine, psychiatry, gerontology, social work, agriculture, urbanology, business and public administration, jurisprudence, criminology, dentistry, nursing, and health, sports and recreation. The five value sciences chosen are intended to serve as significant examples.

1. Aesthetics

Aesthetics is the science inquiring into beauty and ugliness, and into art, that is, fine art. Both inquiries involve understanding aesthetic experience. So let us consider three questions: 1. What is aesthetic experience? 2. What are beauty and ugliness? 3. What is art?

A. Aesthetic Experience.

"Experience is 'aesthetic' when it is enjoyed as complete in itself" (Bahm, 1958, 837). "Aesthetic experience consists in intuition of intrinsic value" (Bahm, 1965, 109). All intuition of enjoyment and suffering is aesthetic experience. So understood, aesthetic experience is more common than commonly supposed. Most experiences have aesthetic aspects, even though these may pass unnoticed because attention is focused on other aspects.

A careful aesthetician will distinguish between the aesthetic and the beautiful, even though all beauty is aesthetic, and between the aesthetic and the ugly, even though all ugliness is aesthetic. Beauty, as we shall note, requires an object, whereas merely aesthetic experience does not. A person may enjoy dazed feelings (during inebriation, post-orgasmic contentment, or falling asleep when exhausted) without attention to objects. Hindu yogins, idealizing Nirguna Brahman as objectless aesthetic awareness, seek to eliminate all objects and to achieve pure aesthetic experience.

B. Beauty and Ugliness.

"Beauty," says hedonist George Santayana, "is constituted by the objectification of pleasure. It is pleasure objectified "(Santayana, 1986, 53). "Organicism agrees, except that it extends objectification of feeling (empathy or *einfühlung*) to include feelings of enthusiasm, satisfaction, contentment, and organic enjoyment" (Bahm, 1968, 452). Beauty exists whenever a person objectifies feelings of enjoyment or projects them as if in an object. The objects may be natural or artificial.

Among the natural objects are those enjoyed in dreams, including daydreams, those projected as ideals, whether for the next meal or as a life goal, those other persons appearing as worthy, including infants, and those visions commanding our awe, such as a shimmering sea, a glowing sunset, or a brilliant rainbow. Among the artificial objects are those created by artists intending to produce experiences of beauty in observers and all of those useful things produced by artisans when interpreted naively as embodying a satisfying usefulness. Whenever you use a tool and enjoy experiencing your skill while using it efficiently as a reliable instrument, you often identify the intrinsic goodness that you feel with the instrumental goodness of your tool. For the skillful carpenter, golfer, or motorcyclist, an efficient hammer, golf club, or motorcycle is a thing of beauty, quite apart from, or in addition to, any artistic decorations on it.

Ugliness, as the projected feelings of suffering into an object, natural or artificial, may be almost as common as beauty. Certainly aestheticians, as well as artists, need to be conscious of ugliness as well as beauty. An aesthetician, as a scientist, who does not have an adequate theory of ugliness, remains deficient. Some general types of beauty and ugliness exist. Distinctions are sometimes made between the pretty, the charming, the quaint, the graceful, the sublime, the tragic, and the grotesque. These too should be investigated thoroughly.

C. Art.

"Art is anything man-made; fine art is art intended, by either maker or appreciator, to be capable of producing experiences of beauty or ugliness under suitable circumstances. Thus, art involves instruments and control of instruments which may serve as instrumental values yielding intrinsic values. Fine art involves intention to make or modify some instrument, the making ('creativity') activity, the instrument made or modified, and appreciation (intuition of intrinsic value, i.e., beauty or ugliness), even if only by the maker" (Bahm, 1968, 453).

Although the aesthetician has the task of distinguishing different kinds of fine arts and of generalizing about each, help must come from specialists in each of the arts. The number of arts seems endless and continually growing. Yet some general types have already appeared, and theories about their natures already have long histories. The following list of kinds of art is incomplete. It is presented for the purpose of revealing the extensiveness of the problems facing aestheticians as scientists.

The major fine arts include: (a) Graphic arts (drawing, painting, printing, engraving, photography). (b) Plastic arts (sculpture, carving, casting, glass blowing, hammered work, pottery, bookbinding, hair dressing, furniture making, sand castles, snow people, plastic surgery, flower arrangement, balloon blowing). (c) Musical arts (vocal, instrumental, and combinations). (d) Architectural arts (homes, cathedrals, skyscrapers, bridges, monuments, ships, airplanes, automobiles, fountains, fences, gates). (e) Landscape design (gardens, parks, malls). (f) Literary arts (novels, poetry, biography, editorials, news articles, features, books). (g) Dramatic arts (drama, dance, ballet, pageants, puppets, burlesque, acrobatics, oratory, balls, weddings, movies). (h) Culinary arts (salads, roasts, cakes, candies, wines, dinners, banquets, menus). (i) Commercial arts (advertising in periodicals, newspapers, television, movies, signs, and office and department store design and furnishings). (j) Computer arts.

The foregoing survey neglects the minor arts, such as costumery, jewelry making, tattooing, and deportment, which many do not consider minor, and some still more major arts, such as the art of living, city planning, and world modeling. The arts as subject matters for scientific investigation are endless.

Since fine art is not only made but also judged, a field of artistic criticism has developed. This field includes many varieties of literary criticism, musical criticism, dramatic criticism, criticism of painting and sculpture, and criticisms for each of the other arts. The aesthetician as scientist has a large range of arts to understand a large range of artistic criticisms to understand. Problems of seeking most reliable standards for judging arts are complicated by views of special-interest groups and ideological sectarian doctrines. Some critics are elitists, claiming that only geniuses can create and appreciate true art. Some critics are democratic and judge art by its popular appeal. Marxists relate art to political economy and evaluate its relevance accordingly. "There is no disputing abut tastes" is quoted often by those who enjoy disputation and by those who abandon efforts to treat fine art scientifically.

My view is that, if we want to, we can investigate much in each art and in art generally by means of scientific attitudes and methods: "Is a universal science of aesthetics possible? Yes. ...The aesthetic consists in intuition of intrinsic value. Beauty consists in objectification of intrinsic goodness. Art consists in the production of, maintenance of, and appreciation of, instruments made or molded for the purpose of producing experiences of beauty. Since everyone experiences goodness, beauty and art, the data for an adequate science of aesthetics are not distant or esoteric" (Bahm, 1972, 3-7).

2. Ethics

The science of ethics, which inquires into oughtness and rightness, is a value science because oughtness and rightness are defined in terms of values. "Oughtness consists in the power which an apparently greater good has over an apparently lesser good...in compelling our choices" (Bahm, 1974a, 135). Without apparent goodness, we have no oughtness. "Acts are right because they are intended to produce the best results for one's self in the long run" (Bahm, 1947, 266). Without intended goodness, or bestness, we have no rightness. Without values, we would have no ethics.

Since a whole volume, *Ethics: The Science of Oughtness*, is meant to be paired with this volume on values, the reader is referred to it for further evidence of ethics as a value science.

3. Religiology

Reluctance to accept the name, "religiology," for scientific studies of religion has sources in adherents to religions reluctant to submit their revealed and revered doctrines to scientific investigation. It has sources in scientists unwilling to challenge obsolete religious doctrines and to promote use of scientific methods in this field. It has sources in political leaders, democratic who depend on votes of traditionalists and authoritarian who prefer not to disturb the status quo. Especially in the United States, systematic study of comparative religions, often with the name of history of religions or philosophy of religion, has been under way for many decades. Nations not committed to religious freedom still discourage scientific investigation of religion.

My interest in science and philosophy resulted from early interest in religion. Professional pursuit of the study and teaching of the world's religions forced me to change my conception of religion. Much Western usage defines religion as "belief in God or gods, or some supernatural or superhuman power or powers." But this conception was derived from generalizing hastily on acquaintance with too few religions. When my studies revealed that Jainism and Theravada Buddhism, with millions of adherents in India and South Asian countries, were explicitly atheistic, I was forced to conclude that the prevalent Western definition is mistaken. But if religion is not belief in God, what is it?

Although a study of the history of religions and histories of philosophies yielded a plethora of alternative definitions, my method was that of studying most of the world's religions to discover what they have in common, hoping that awareness of their common characteristics would provide clues to characteristics essential to the nature of religion. My present hypothesis: "Religion consists in concern for the ultimate value of life, and how to attain it, preserve it, and enjoy it" (Bahm, 1964, 16). Doctrines, although they normally contain views about the origin, nature, and future of the universe, humanity, and values, differ widely. But all have some conception of the value of life as a whole, of the ultimate values that make life worth living, and, consequently, some conceptions of means appropriate to achieving such value. This hypothesis is testable by others, by a reexamination of the world's religions, old and new, and any newer ones yet to emerge.

If religion is concern for ultimate values, it is, in a fundamental sense, the most important concern. If so, then should not religiology be the science in which each person is most interested? Unfortunately, identification of religion with increasingly obsolete doctrines has resulted in misconceptions of religion as something we will do away with altogether.[1] But persons are incurably religious, not in the sense of being gullible or superstitious, but in being greatly interested in life's most ultimate values. If oughtness exists whenever you are faced with a choice between alternatives, one of which appears to have greater value than the others, then whenever you are faced with a choice between seeking to achieve a lesser and a greater, more ultimate value, which ought you choose? The greater. Thus your religious values are your most important values, and your religious ethics is your most important ethics.

Religion is both personal and social. Persons and societies often survive or perish because of their religious doctrines and practices. A vital, intelligent religion, with institutions at the stage of efficiency, can be a most valuable national resource. It inspires confidence, loyalty, and cooperation when interdependent political, religious, and personal values support each other. But a nation saddled with an obsolete religion, compelling conformity but performing little constructive service, is crippled by it.

The "separation of church and state" policy, adopted by the United States as a result of the evils of religious wars in Europe, included a policy of religious toleration and religious freedom. It was a wise policy, especially since, among the imported sects, much dogmatism, fanaticism and divisiveness prevailed. This policy has consequences, some bad as well as some good. Separation of sectarian churches from state institutions is a wise policy; but separation of religion from government, when the values of government, especially those providing for security of its citizens, are important parts of the ultimate values of each person, creates a division where there should be a union. A major cause of division between religion and government these days is the division between religions.

"Religion unites; religions divide. Today we have too many religions and not enough religion. The multiplicity of religions has an anti-religious effect. Now, religions are the chief enemy of religion" (Bahm, 1979, 190). The nature of religion, and the natural constructive functions of religion, are researchable subjects. The results of serious, courageous, and persistent scientific investigations into religion can have significant consequences for our national interests. A vital, efficient, reliable religion is a valuable national resource. Religiology, the value science having the task of investigating, should receive appropriate support.

My explorations into the problem of choosing a better religion have led to my proposing seventeen "principles for choosing" among alternative world views (Bahm, 1992, ch. 34). Now that the values of interdisciplinary research are being more widely recognized, I hope that its continuing development may lead eventually to significant consequences for philosophy and religion. "Interdisciplinology promises us the prospect of a truer and more adequate world view than has been possible heretofore" (Bahm, 1980, 35).

4. Economics

Economics is the most well-known value science and thus least in need of comment here. Economics as a science inquires into wealth and income (and illth and expenditures), of goods and services, their production, exchange, distribution and consumption, and all of the problems involved with them.

Economics has contributed to and benefitted from general theories of value. Yet difficulties with traditional theories and the powerful but insidious influence of "value-free" philosophies of science held by many emulated physical scientists have motivated some economists to make this value science value-free. Beginning by taking "wants," based on human desires, and then restricting "wants" to those satisfiable by economic means, economists focused on what satisfied those needs, that is, what is useful or has utility (instrumental value). Accumulation of data about quantities and kinds of production, consumption, distribution, and exchange of things having utility led to locating economic value primarily in "exchange value," something obviously quantitative.

Finally, after huge increases in the role of money in exchange, some economists tried to define economics as the science of price. Here the claimed basis is clearly quantitative, and any distant connections with desires and satisfactions (intrinsic values) can be ignored. Price is often influenced by cornering markets, stock manipulation, inflation, central bank interest rate adjustment, political decisions, and other technical factors in economic processes. While taking these decisive factors increasingly into account, some economists became more negligent of, even indifferent to, the ultimate bases of the whole economic enterprise. "The economist is not concerned with ends as such" because "the economist is entirely neutral as between ends" (Robbins, 1948, 24, 25).

This view is mistaken. The reason for the mistake is the failure to establish axiology as a recognized and reliable science. Establishing axiology as a recognized science helps reestablish economics as a value science on a sound value basis. The more complexly interdependent the peoples of the world become, the more complex our economic processes become, and the greater the need for theoretical soundness, to have economics soundly grounded in reliable axiology (Bahm, 1979, ch. 7).

5. Policy Sciences

The policy sciences are, in a fundamental sense, parts of political science. But there is much more in political science, which inquires into government, than the policy sciences, which concentrate on problems involved in making group decision, public or private. The policy sciences are multidisciplinary in that factors dealt with primarily in other sciences, such as economic, social, ecological, and educational, are deliberately taken into account when formulating decisions.[2] The role of values in policy decisions is often recognized (Jacobs, 1962, 1-38).

However, the status of the policy sciences among the sciences is still questioned by many. The reason is the failure of policy scientists to be sufficiently multidisciplinary and interdisciplinary. One of the disciplines most seriously neglected is ethics. Every policy question is an ethical question. Every policy decision is an ethical decision. But, in spite of increasing awareness of the presence of ethical issues in policy matters, almost no awareness of the possibilities of and need for developing and utilizing ethics as a science exists.

Those most eager to improve the scientific reliability of the policy sciences look not to ethics but to mathematics, and they have explored mathematical conditions of decisions. Mathematics is a tool that should be used whenever it can be useful. But policy decisions are primarily ethical decisions, not mathematical decisions. As long as policy scientists are guided by a mistaken philosophy of science, they are misguided and can expect continuing lack of confidence in their reliability. Loss of confidence in the scientific community is currently deplored by L.M. Branscomb: "The situation is particularly bad in the area for science for decision-making. ...We have few institutions within which all the appropriate skills can be directed at major problem areas..., they do not perform the needed interdisciplinary research" (Branscomb, 1977, 850).

Six

THE SCIENCE OF VALUES

Two tasks have been set for the present chapter: To show that axiology is already established as a science. To inquire into what remains to be done to gain recognition of its establishment in the minds of others.

1. An Established Science

The history of value theory is intricately intermeshed with the history of other value sciences and of other philosophical sciences, so a review of these is needed to reveal its origins and developments. But it does have its own history, even if some of its origins are recent.

A. Axiology.

Value problems have plagued humanity from our beginnings. All survival problems are value problems.

I do not know when value theory first occurred. Early Greek philosophers, to whom many sciences recognize indebtedness, formulated theories of value that made lasting contributions which influenced thinkers from time to time. Aristotle opens his *Nicomachean Ethics* by saying that the good is "that at which all things aim. ...If there is some end of the things we do, which we desire for its own sake...clearly this must be...the chief good" (Ross, 1925, v.9, 1094). Hedonism, the theory that intrinsic good consists in pleasant feeling, was already well-developed and widely debated by Greek thinkers. Plato eulogized the Idea of the Good as the eternal source of all existing goodness, including the goodness embodied in all particular things, and also the primary source of all other beings, as far as their natures are concerned. Plato's influence on Christian theology, through Plotinus who identified the Good with The One as the source of all other beings which are as deficient in goodness as they are deficient in being when they become more plurified, and through Augustine, has caused many to identify value theory with theology.

With Aquinas and Calvin, God is omnibenevolent and perfect goodness. The Christian solution to the problem of evil, after rejecting as heretical the doctrine of two Gods, one good and one evil, continues to be unsatisfactory, because it involves an all-powerful, all-good, and all-good-willing God who created a world filled with evil. Dissenters who reject theology often abandon value theory as identified with the rejected theology.

Modern axiology is exemplified in the writings of Jeremy Bentham (1748-1832) and John Stuart Mill (1806-1873). "Jeremy Bentham's 'calculus of pleasures' was, in its way, a first form of an axiology in value matters" (Ehrenfels, 1897). Mill, who provided modern science with one of its most systematic introductions to inductive and experimental methods (Mill, 1843), extended Hedonistic pleasures to include mental pleasures as having superior quality (Mill, 1863, ch. 2).

Value theory in the late nineteenth century was especially indebted to Franz Brentano (Brentano, 1874), who emphasized presentational immediacy as the foundation for value judgments, Alexius Meinong (Meinong, 1984), who showed how value theory, when keyed to our emotional responses, explains value experiences of all kinds, and Christian von Ehrenfels (Werkmeister, 1973, vii, 32), who explored both desires and feelings as bases for values and concluded that desires are more foundational (Eaton, 1930).

The name "axiology," although an English equivalent of two Greek terms, was not used extensively until the beginning of the twentieth century. It appeared in the works of Paul Lapie, *Logique de la Volunté*, Paris: F. Alcan, 1902, and Eduard von Hartmann, *Grundriss der Axiologie*, Bad Sachsa im Harz: H. Haacke, 1908. In 1909, Wilbur Marshall Urban published *Valuation, Its Nature and Laws*, a first major work in the United States. "We not only *feel* the value of objects, but we evaluate those objects and ultimately the feelings of value themselves" (Urban, 1909, 1).

Recent preeminent American axiologists and their major works, chronologically arranged, include:

D. W. Prall. *A Study in the Theory of Value*. Berkeley, Cal.: University of California Publications, 1921.

Ralph Barton Perry. *General Theory of Value*. New York: Longmans, 1926.

DeWitt H. Parker. *Human Values*. New York: Harper, 1931.

John R. Reid. *A Theory of Value*. New York: Scribner's, 1938.

John Dewey. *Theory of Valuation.* Chicago: University of Chicago Press, 1939.

Ray Lepley. *Verifiability of Value.* New York: Columbia University Press, 1944.

Clarence I. Lewis. *An Analysis of Knowledge and Valuation.* LaSalle, Ill.: Open Court, 1946.

A. L. Hilliard. *The Forms of Value: The Extension of a Hedonistic Axiology.* New York: Columbia University Press, 1950.

Ralph K. White. *Value Analysis: The Nature and Use of Its Methods.* Glen Gardner, N. J.: Society for the Psychological Study of Social Issues, 1951.

E. W. Hall. *What Is Value?* New York: Humanities Press, 1952.

Stephen C. Pepper. *The Source of Value.* Berkeley: University of California Press, 1958.

DeWitt H. Parker. *The Philosophy of Value.* Ann Arbor, Mich.: University of Michigan Press, 1957.

C. West Churchman. *Prediction and Optimal Decision: The Philosophical Issues of a Science of Values.* Chicago: University of Chicago Press, 1961.

Risieri Frondizi., *What Is Value? An Introduction to Axiology.* Englewood Cliffs, N.J.: Prentice-Hall, 1963.

D. W. Gotshalk. *Patterns of Good and Evil.* LaSalle. Ill.: Open Court, 1963.

Robert S. Hartman. *The Structure of Value: Foundations of a Scientific Axiology.* Urbana, Ill.: University of Illinois Press, 1967.

Peter Caws. *Science and the Theory of Value.* New York: Random House, 1967.

Nicholas Rescher. *Introduction to Value Theory.* Englewood Cliffs, N.J.: Prentice-Hall, 1969.

Erwin Laszlo and James B. Wibur, eds. *Human Value and Natural Sciences.* New York: Gordon and Breach, 1970.

J. N. Findlay. *Axiological Ethics.* London: Macmillan, 1970.

Robin Attfield. *A Theory of Value and Obligation.* London: Croom Helm, 1987.

Sander H. Lee, ed. *Inquiries into Values.* Lewiston, N.Y.: Edwin Mellen Press, 1988.

Axiologists organized the American Society for Value Inquiry in 1970, and the International Society for Value Inquiry in 1988. *The Journal of Value Inquiry* was founded in 1967, reporting "current research in axiology." *The Philosopher's Index*, begun in 1967, records and classifies philosophical books and articles. Its first eleven volumes list 2 items under "axiology" and 744 more under "values." Its *Retrospective Index*, from 1940, lists 50 titles under "axiology" and almost 1,200 under "values."

Established as a science in its own right, axiology has contributed to and has been contributed to by many other sciences. Much of the delay in recognizing axiology as a distinct science is due to the incorporation of its basic problems into the problems of other sciences. Some of the research in these other sciences has been axiological research even though the distinctness of axiological research was not recognized. Identification of axiological problems as problems in these other sciences has contributed to confusion about values and to reluctance to recognize the problems as constituting a distinct science. Thus, although the following sketches of other sciences is kept brief, their contributions to axiology are often significant.

B. Aesthetics.

Aesthetics as the science of beauty and ugliness is concerned with objectified intuited enjoyment (intrinsic good) and suffering (intrinsic evil). As such, aesthetics as a science deals directly with axiological problems. Aesthetics is also a science inquiring into the arts as instruments for producing such intrinsic values. Once questions are raised about art, the many arts, artistic creativity, artistic appreciation, and social, economic and political aspects of the arts, then aesthetics is involved in problems distinctly its own. These do not cease to be axiological questions to the extent that intrinsic values are involved. But the additional problems, each with its peculiarities, requires additional, and often different, principles of explanation. Although we speak of aesthetics as a science, the name also covers a whole range of sciences, since each of the kinds of art, such as music, literature, architecture, drama, and even each of the constituent arts, such as violin music, has a sufficiently specific nature to warrant calling its investigation a science.

Authors of the following books penetrate axiological problems and contribute to the development of axiology as a science.

John Bascom. *Aesthetics: Or The Science of Beauty*. Boston: Crosby and Nichols, 1862.

Eduard von Hartmann. *Aesthetic.* Leipzig: H. Haacke, 1886.

Bernard Bosanquet. *A History of Aesthetic.* New York: Macmillan, 1892.

George Santayana. *The Sense of Beauty.* New York: Scribner's, 1896.

Ethel B. Puffer. *The Psychology of Beauty.* Boston: Houghton, 1905.

Kate Gordon. *Esthetics.* New York: Holt, 1909.

Vernon Lee. *The Beautiful: An Introduction to Psychological Analysis.* London: Cambridge University Press, 1913.

DeWitt H. Parker. *The Principles of Aesthetics.* Boston: Silver, Burdett, 1920.

Henry S. Langfeld. *The Aesthetic Attitude.* New York: Harcourt Brace, 1920

Laurence Buermeyer. *The Aesthetic Experience.* Merion, Pa.: Barnes Foundation, 1924.

Samuel Alexander. *Beauty and Other Forms of Value.* London: Macmillan, 1933.

William A. Hammond. *A Bibliography of Aesthetics and the Philosophy of Fine Arts from 1900 to 1932.* New York: Longmans, 1934.

Milton C. Nahm. *Aesthetic Experience and Its Presuppositions.* New York: Harper, 1946.

Monroe C. Beardsley. *Aesthetics: Problems in the Philosophy of Criticism.* New York: Harcourt Brace, 1958.

Harold Osborne. *Aesthetics.* London: Oxford University Press, 1972.

Stefan Morawski. *Inquiries into the Fundamentals of Aesthetics.* Cambridge, Mass.: MIT Press, 1974.

D. E. Berlyne. *Studies in the New Experimental Aesthetics.* Washington: Hemisphere Publishing Corporation, 1974.

Theodor W. Adorno, Gretel Adorno, Rolf Tiedmann, eds. *Aesthetic Theory.* London: Routledge & Kegan Paul, 1984.

Hugo A. Meynell. *The Nature of Aesthetic Value.* Albany, N.Y.: S.U.N.Y. Press, 1986.

George Dickie, et. al., eds. *Aesthetics: A Critical Anthology.* New York: Saint Martin's Press, 1989.

Marcia M. Eaton. *Basic Issues in Aesthetics.* Belmont, Cal.: Wadsworth Publishing Co., 1988.

Göran Hermerén. *The Nature of Aesthetic Qualities*. Melbourne, Fla.: Krieger Publishing Co., 1988.

Frederick Turner. *Beauty: The Value of Values*. Charlottesville, Va.: University Press of Virginia, 1992.

The *Journal of Aesthetics and Art Criticism* started in 1941 and the American Society for Aesthetics in 1942. The *Bulletin International d'Esthétique*, published by the Institute of Aesthetics, The Netherlands, began in 1967.

C. Ethics.

Ethics is one of the oldest sciences, competing with physics and astronomy for earliest origin. Confucius, who studied the political practices of several courts of his time and of earlier times, observed differing ethical practices producing differing results. His generalizations remain among the soundest ever proposed, and must be reckoned with by anyone who would improve upon them (Bahm, 1969, 15-19).

Aristotle produced three works on ethics (Ross, 1925). The *ics* in both physics and ethics originated early Greek times. One of the first textbooks to come to my attention, Theodore Delaguna's *Introduction to the Science of Ethics* (Delaguna, 1914), supported my confidence that establishment of ethics as a universally reliable science is possible and actualizable as soon as we devote efforts needed in bringing it about.

Ethical reasoning involves reasons for choosing between goods, or evils, and thus involves justification of choices in terms of goods or evils. Much of the motive for understanding values is that ethical choices can be validated only when their ultimate value bases are clear. Such clarity existed already in Aristotle: "The good [is] that at which all things aim" (Ross, 1925, 1094).

Ethics is concerned with oughtness. Oughtness consists in the power that an apparently greater good has over an apparently lesser good in compelling our choices. Every choice is thus an ethical choice. Every decision is an ethical decision. So values, goods and bads, are involved in every decision. Every decision made by a physicist, physician, engineer, and accountant, as well as by parent and teacher, is thus ethical, and thereby also axiological.

Research in each scientific field, such as medicine, law, psychiatry, forestry, and aviation, dealing with problems involving ethical ingredients often produces workable solutions having implications for axiology, even when these are not fully understood. They provide resources for regarding axiology as a science.

Additional evidence of contributions of ethics to the establishment of axiology as a science will be assembled in chapter 6 of my *Ethics: The Science of Oughtness*.

D. Religiology.

Religion as concern for the intrinsic values of life as a whole, can be studied scientifically. Hence the name "religiology." The Society for the Scientific Study of Religion, was founded in 1949, and its official *Journal for the Scientific Study of Religion*, has been published since 1961. *Zygon: Journal of Religion and Science*, published by the Chicago Center for Religion and Science since 1966, provides a forum for "thinkers who attempt to integrate contemporary scientific knowledge and basic human values."

My answer to how to investigate religion scientifically and in what sense religious values are higher values appears in my *Philosophy: An Introduction* (Bahm, 1953, ch. 25), and my conception of religion, after extensive research, is presented in my *The World's Living Religions* (Bahm, 1964, ch. 1).

E. Economics.

Economics is a value science accepted by the scientific community. It is essentially a value science. The history of economic thought is permeated with value theory. Although economics is concerned primarily with instrumental values, called "utilities," their grounding in intrinsic values is often recognized. "The real price of everything," said Adam Smith, "is the toil and trouble [intrinsic evil] of acquiring it" (Haney, 1911, 202).

Labor theories of value have given way to much more complex analyses of the kinds of factors involved in the production of goods. International linkage of multifactor computerized data bank networks provides economists with intricate data generalization possibilities that continue to be utterly amazing (Bahm, 1979, 208-230).

How does economic science serve to establish axiology? We have many examples:

Irving Fisher. *Mathematical Investigations in the Theory of Value and Price*. Fairfield, N.J.: A. M. Kelley, 1892.

Hannah Robie Sewall. *The Theory of Value Before Adam Smith*. New York: A. M. Kelley, 1901.

Edward Chamberlain. *Towards a More General Theory of Value*. New York: Oxford University Press, 1957.

Kenneth E. Boulding. "Some Contributions of Economics to the General Theory of Values." *Philosophy of Science*. 23:1 (1958): 1-14.

Kenneth Arrow. *Social Choice and Individual Values*, 2nd ed. New York: Wiley, 1963.

Sidney Hook. *Human Values and Economic Policy*. New York: New York University Press, 1967.

Robin Niell. *A New Theory of Value: The Canadian Economics of H. A. Ennis*. Toronto: University of Toronto Press, 1972.

Jeffrey T. Young. *Classical Theories of Value: From Smith to Sraffa*. Boulder, Colo.: Westview Press, 1978.

Mark Blaug. *The Cambridge Revolution, Success or Failure: A Critical Analysis of Cambridge Theories of Value and Distribution*. London: Institute of Economic Affairs, 1974.

D. P. Mahesward, ed. *Towards a Theory of Value: Focus on David Recardo*. Bhopal: Progress Publishers, 1978.

Giovanni A. Caravale and Domencio A. Tosato. *Ricardo and the Theory of Value, Distribution, and Growth*. London: Routledge, 1980.

John Eatwell and Murray Milgate, eds. *Keynes's Economics and Theory of Value and Distribution*. New York: Oxford University Press, 1983.

Peter M. Lichtenstein. *An Introduction to Post-Keynsian and Marxian Theories of Value and Price*. Armonk, N. Y.: M. E. Sharpe, 1983.

F. Biology.

Feelings of enjoyment and suffering constituting intrinsic values have bases in biological evolution and depend on physiological organs adapted to serving needs for surviving and acting intelligently.

For example, "the instincts are the prime movers of all human activity; by the conative or impulsive force of some instinct (or of some habit derived from an instinct), every train of thought, however cold and passionless it may seem, is borne along towards its end and every bodily activity is initiated and sustained" (McDougall, 1921, 45). Instincts are sources of desires generating the enjoyments and sufferings existing as the intrinsic goods and evils investigated by axiology.

Psychobiologist R. W. Sperry says: "Perhaps more than any other single development, the advance of the last half-century in our understanding of the neural mechanisms of mind and conscious awareness clear the way for a rational approach to the realm of values (Sperry, 1974, 18). Sociologist Edward O. Wilson says: "The question that science is now in a position to answer is the very origin and meaning of human values, from which all ethical pronouncements and much political practice flow" (Wilson, 1976, 1153). Intrinsic goods and evils are feelings of enjoyment and suffering involving secretions and neurological reactions that physiologists as scientists understand. Their contributions are foundational to axiology.

G. Psychology.

No problem is more central to psychology than understanding feelings and emotions. What are pleasure and pain, joy and sorrow, love and hate, confidence and fear, pride and humiliation? All involve feelings of enjoyment and suffering, with varying intensities and durations. Each may contribute to desires and participate in shaping ideals of action and achievement felt as good. "Emotions constitute the primary motivational system for human beings" (Izard, 1977, 3). Axiology is indebted to psychology for exploring feelings and emotions in great detail (Arnold, 1970).

Recent articles and books:

L. L. Thurstone. "The Measurement of Values." *Psychological Review* 61 (1953): 47-58.

J. E. Schorr. "The Development of a Test to Measure the Intensity of Values." *Journal of Educational Psychology* 44 (1953): 266-274.

William Dukes. "Psychological Studies of Values." The *Psychological Bulletin.* 52 (1955): 24-50.

Robert F. Creegan. "Recent Trends in the Psychology of Values." *Present-Day Psychology.* Ed. by A. A. Roback. New York: Philosophical Library, 1955, 949-960.

H. J. Muller. "Values, Scientific Method, and Psychoanalysis."
Psychiatry 127 (1958): 625-627.

Magda B. Arnold. *Feelings and Emotions*. New York: Academic
Press, 1970.

Carroll Izard. *Human Emotions*. New York: Plenum Press, 1977.

Leonard Cirillo and Seymour Wapner. *Value Presuppositions in
Human Development*. Hillsdale, N.J.: Lawrence Erlbaum Associates,
1981.

Jack George Thompson. *The Psychology of Emotions*. New York:
Plenum Press, 1988.

H. Sociology.

Concerns ranging from interpersonal relations to organized groups and
cultures involve understanding the roles of feelings of enjoyment and
suffering at every stage. Feelings constantly contribute to social
activities, and understanding them is needed for understanding society.
And the various kinds of social activity, ranging from participating in
primary groups to institutions of community, national, and world
dimensions, influence the kinds and amounts of feelings of enjoyment
and suffering in persons.

Sociology includes concerns for a good life, and when applied in
practice it involves many kinds of social welfare. The social sciences
emphasize investigation of instrumental values needed to support
actualization of intrinsic values. Social values are often conceived in
terms of cultural ideals and standards of behavior having existence
outside of persons; actually their ultimate basis is located in the
feelings of persons. Axiological foundations of sociology are implicit
throughout its investigations. The ways in which values function in
society serve as problems for axiological research.

Some recent books:

Ervin Laszlo and James B. Wilbur, eds. *Value Theory in Philosophy
and the Social Sciences*. New York: Gordon and Breach Science
Publishers, 1973.

Theodore D. Kemper. *A Social Interactive Theory of Emotions*.
New York: Wiley, 1978.

Timo Airaksinen. *From Subjective Welfare to Social Value: Axiology
in Methodological and Philosophical Perspective*. Helsinki: Suomalainen
Tiedeakatemia, 1979.

Tracy B. Strong. *Aesthetics and the Search for Political Authority.*
Boulder, Colo.: Westview Press, 1993.

I. Anthropology.

Ruth Benedict, author of *Patterns of Culture*, "understood that, when
we talk about morals specifically or values in general, we are talking
about feelings.... To study ethos is to study the emotional logic through
an interpretive description of that life in terms of values" (Wilk, 1991,
222).

Studies in the mores of ancient and contemporary cultures provide
data which axiologists must examine and evaluate. Although
anthropologists are not primarily axiologists, their functions include
recording primitive myths about persons and tribes and their values.
Vast libraries and museums of anthropological data are part of the
data banks available for axiologists. Increasingly numerous and detailed
research in many areas have implication for value theory, both
challanging and supporting axiological investigations.

2. What Remains to Be Done?

The second task of the present chapter is to inquire into what
remains to be done to gain recognition of the establishment of axiology
as a science in the minds of others. The others chosen for this task are
members of the scientific community in the United States, although the
problem has become world-wide to the extent that predominant
attitudes among scientists in the United States are shared in other
countries.

Although the primary problems of axiology and ethics are distinct,
they interdepend, and any adequate solution must take into account
such interdependence. I propose recognition of two distinguishsble
sciences, axiology and ethics. Some persons may be persuaded to
accept one, or the other, but not both, as sciences. My proposal
involves accepting both. My proposal exists at two levels. At its most
general level, it aims to overcome the exclusion of axiology and ethics
from science, without specifying which theories are acceptable as
scientific. At its most specific level, it aims to achieve acceptance of
axiology and ethics as conceived and expressed in this book. Many of
those who already accept axiology and ethics as sciences do not accept

(because not acquainted with) and many will not accept my particular conceptions. Both of these complexities deserve consideration.

A. Axiology and Ethics.

Clear distinction between goodness and oughtness is needed for understanding each. Inquiry into each is a distinct kind of problem and constitutes a distinct science.

Some goods exist without oughts. A person may formulate a theory of the nature of goodness without involving a theory of oughtness. So axiology, as the science inquiring into the nature of goodness and badness, can exist without immediately involving ethics.

But all oughts, I believe, depend on goods. I reject as mistaken those deontological theories claiming that duty (oughtness) exists by nature as prior to goodness and determines the nature of goodness. An adequate theory of oughtness does involve an adequate theory of goodness. So ethics, as the science inquiring into oughtness, does immediately involve axiology, even though some inquirers may achieve considerable clarity about oughtness without having done so regarding goodness.

Axiology and ethics interdepend. To be fully adequate, axiology needs to know how its values function as determiners of oughts, obligations, and duties. To be fully adequate, ethics needs to know how its oughts are founded in intrinsic values, those constituting the ultimate bases for ethical appeals. Clarity about both the partial independence and the intimate interdependence of axiology and ethics is needed for establishing them as sciences. So, promoting such clarity, wherever it does not exist, is something that remains to be done.

B. General and Particular.

Two distinct tasks, which appear to me to be interdependent, remain.

i. *General.* One has to do with overcoming the mistaken resistance in the scientific community to accepting axiology and ethics as sciences. The scientific community in the United States includes the officers and members of the American Association for the Advancement of Science, the National Science Foundation, the National Research Council, the National Academy of Sciences, and the National Science Board. In 1975 I began prodding H. Guyford Stever, Director of the

National Science Foundation. Responding to his article, "Whither the NSF?" (Stever, *Science*, 189 [1975]: 246-268), I asked him why NSF had failed to recognize axiology as a science. Stever replied that "we at the Foundation are aware of a great deal of work which has been done in the area of the scientific study of values over the last several decades. ...NSF has not only supported studies of human values from the perspectives of all of the appropriate scientific disciplines, but...it is our intent to continue supporting both disciplinary and interdisciplinary work in this area at a significant level in the future."[1] When I pointed out that axiology has not been mentioned among "all of the appropriate scientific disciplines" (which included "sociology, social psychology, economics, advanced environmental research, exploratory research and problem assessment, and the history and philosophy of science"), and asked "Why not?"[2] reply came in a letter from Robert J. Baum stating that "we cannot give you a direct 'yes' or 'no' answer."[3]

After the National Science Board, meeting 3-4 February 1977, "unanimously approved the program policies for the Ethics and Values in Science and Technology Program,"[4] I wrote to its Chairman, Norman Hackerman, calling "attention to a serious inconsistency in policy proposals. ...The inconsistency of proposing guidelines for scientific research grants relative to ethical and value issues when no scientific bases relative to ethics and values are recognized seems most serious. ...Should not any research needed to establish axiology and ethics as sciences have priority over examining ethical and value issues arising from the conduct of science, so long as ethics and axiology are not yet recognized as sciences?"[5] Chairman Hackerman replied, "Neither the NSF Advisory Committee nor the National Science Board has called for a strictly scientific examination of ethical and value issues."[6]

On 18 November 1977, I wrote Chairman Hackerman, "I request official NSF recognition of axiology and ethics as sciences," after submitting manuscript copies of the present book and of *Ethics the Science of Oughtness* and a copy of *Ethics as a Behavioral Science*.[7] After further correspondence, Chairman Hackerman wrote that the National Science Board at its February meeting "agreed that axiology and ethics are not sciences as set out in section 3(a)1 of the NSF Act of 1950, as amended, and the Act does not indicate that the framers of the law intended to include axiology and ethics among the sciences to be supported by the Foundation."[8] After reading the Act, I replied to Chairman Hackerman, "It is clear that the Act intended to include 'other sciences' which were not specified. The Act does not specifically exclude any science. The Act does not specify 'behavioral sciences,' but NSF funding of research in the behavioral sciences occurs. If 'NSF has already invested more than a million dollars in scientific research into values in one year,'[9] then how can the Board reach an 'agreement' that axiology, the proper name for research into values, is not a science?"[10]

What remains to be done? Reversal of the Board's opinion. A major part of the problem appears to be the virtual stranglehold that Logical Positivism as a philosophy of science has over the opinions of a majority of American scientists, even when they are not aware of this condition. The falsity of its assumptions and conclusions has been demonstrated again and again.[11] But those accepting them have not been listening.[12] The value-free conception of science conveniently relieves scientists of responsibility for scientific investigation of values. But accumulating crises, caused partly by unanticipated effects of science and technology (for example, overpopulation, pollution of air, water, and land, rapid exhaustion of irreplaceable resources, technological unemployment), have caused public concern. Many in the scientific community are disturbed by increasing expressions of unfavorable attitudes toward science. But their response, thus far, which gives no evidence of willingness to challenge mistaken value-free assumptions, has been, first, to spend more money researching the value effects of science and technology and, more recently, to try to polish their public image with a popular periodical, *Science 80*.

Responding to political pressures resulting from such criticisms, the scientific community has agreed to examine and evaluate (but not to use the value-laden term "evaluate"; "value-free" scientists cannot consistently "evaluate," so they must "assess," which is evaluating while pretending not to involve values) the effects of science and technology. Political response has resulted in the U.S. Congress establishing an Office of Technology Assessment (later abandoned), in extensive hearings in House and Senate Committees on Science and Technology, and in the establishment of a National Commission on Research. A recent NSF program announcement, *Ethics and Values in Science and Technology*, requires projects to have "significant ethical value or content," and invites applicant interest in "ethical issues and value assumptions in decision making processes involving science and technology," but insists that the program does not support "projects whose principal aim is to clarify ethical theory as it applies to science and technology...."

In spite of growing numbers of scientists questioning value-free assumptions and growing demands that scientists come to terms with the value nature of science and technology, the predominating view apparently refuses to question these assumptions seriously and thus to admit axiology and ethics as sciences. Much remains to be done.

ii. *Particular.* Many theories about the nature of values and of oughtness exist. Even if axiology and ethics were recognized as "appropriate" fields, and all of those many theories were recognized as legitimate hypotheses, the task of deciding which among them is the most adequate would remain. My main reason for seeking to have axiology and ethics recognized as sciences is so that the search for a most adequate theory can begin and then be pursued more vigorously. But absence of recognition of these as general sciences by the National Science Board and others in the scientific community does not prevent search for a more adequate theory. A main part of my purpose in preparing this book and my *Ethics: The Science of Oughtness* is also to state, at least in a preliminary way, a particular theory about values and a particular theory about oughtness and rightness, which have implications for theories explaining rights, justice, conscience, self, society, and culture. If they can be demonstrated to be the most adequate theories, establishment of their acceptance should reduce resistance in the scientific community to recognizing axiology and ethics as sciences.

NOTES

Two WHAT IS SCIENCE?

1. Distinguishing between "apparent objects," that is, objects as they appear in experience, and "real objects," that is, things judged to exist in ways that do not appear, and exist whether or not they appear, I choose not to define science in a way that insists on belief in "real things." Personally, however, I do believe that limiting science to apparent objects not only restricts it unduly, but also constitutes a serious deficiency handicapping scientific investigation. Thus, for me, the willingness to be objective includes a willingness to be realistic.

2. Such law has been interpreted either as timelessly subsisting as eternally real forms (that is Plato's Ideas, or the "facts" of Logical Realists) or as forms essential to minds (that is Kant's principles of "Pure Reason").

3. Extreme realists, those mistakenly believing that objectivity requires complete separation from all subjectivity, are more likely to be unwilling to be changed by their investigations. Such an attitude may have seemed warranted when less adequate conceptions of the nature of things and knowledge prevailed. But today surely they must be condemned as inadequate.

4. The role of doubt in science and its replacement by belief is ably depicted by Charles Sanders Peirce in "The Fixation of Belief," *Popular Science Monthly*, 13 (1877): 1-15.

Three WHAT ARE VALUES?

1. Conflicting conceptions of scales of values function as another source of confusion and unclear thinking about values.

2. This proposal has implications for those theories holding one or the other as more important. For example, Platonism and Neo-Platonism hold that no bad really exists and interpret bad as merely a deficiency of good, and Advaita Vedanta claims that Brahman is pure goodness (<u>ananda</u>) and that all badness is illusory (<u>Maya</u>).

3. For an able account of the "dialectics of the Romantic soul," see Mark J. Temmer, *Time in Rousseau and Kant*, ch. IV. Geneva, Droz, 1958.

4. Existentialism, a current form of Romanticism, locates ultimate reality in each act of will (<u>Existenz</u>), which is supposed to create, spontaneously, its own objects, projects, and hence goals. But intrinsic value is enjoyed when a will is "authentic," that is, does not permit itself to be imposed upon by anything else, either laws, principles, other people, or even one's previous promises. Such a will cannot call for help from any other person or source and remain completely "authentic." Some wills, suffering lack of projects, also suffer lack of willfulness because they cannot provide, out of their own unstructured lives, any goals sufficiently worth while to strive for. Only by contemplating death, or non-existence of will, and judging the nothingness of nonbeing to be worse than its being, can some people continue to suffer the absurdity of life and its evil so conceived. Thus desiring itself is intrinsically good and dread of desirelessness is intrinsically evil.

5. Notice may be taken of similarities between the series of stages in coital accomplishment, the stages in a life cycle, and the stages in the scientific method relative to successive prevalence of each of our four kinds of intrinsic values. Scientific method is initiated when observation, involving sensory stimuli (pleasantly or unpleasantly), generates a problematic attitude involving a desire to solve the problem, which desire then inspires efforts to deal with the problem, efforts that may range from earnest interest to zealous enthusiasm, and even persist as manic compulsiveness, and which desire is felt as being satisfied when the desired hypothesis is being formulated and tested. When a thesis is communicated and accepted as a "scientific fact," that is, is no longer questioned, but is utilized in solving other problems, the scientist achieves a feeling of contentment relative to that problem. Far from being "value-free," science is value-saturated, and if enjoyment of each of the four kinds of intrinsic value is essential to each of the four or five stages of the scientific method, then science is inherently dependent upon the production and experiencing of all four kinds of intrinsic value and their presence successively in the successive stages in the scientific process. How the four kinds supplement each other can be seen again in this example.

Four KNOWLEDGE OF VALUES

1. Considering the foundational importance of intuition in knowledge, including all scientific knowledge, any neglect of epistemology as a basic science by the scientific community is serious. Considering the amount of basic research remaining to be done, and the fundamental need for having sound foundations for knowledge, including knowledge on which national security is based, persons responsible for guarding our national interests should be deeply concerned about promoting such research.

2. Since so much has been written about "mystical intuition," supposedly exemplified in clairvoyance, telepathy, and extrasensory perception, some reference to it should be made here. Since my experience has yielded no evidence that I have ever had a mystical intuition, I omit it from consideration. Others have capacities that I do not have, more sensitive olfactory sensation, for example. So I must remain open-minded regarding such possible kinds of knowing. But I have nothing to offer that may contribute to understanding it.

3. Following Plato, who idealized concepts of types of being as eternal forms, called IDEAS, many today still hold that the forms embodied in particular conceptions as well as those in particular things are eternal (for example, A.N. Whitehead's "eternal objects"). Logical Realists presuppose eternal reality for their formal propositions and for the "facts," which are also eternal forms, that "make them true." Many mathematicians and users of mathematics do the same. But anyone examining the difficulties, metaphysical, physical, or physiological, of having eternal forms (existing nowhere yet somehow present or available everywhere) pop into concepts and events, and then out again, magically accommodating each mental and physical occasion, must surely have doubts about the view. Injection of forms of concepts and events from some outside eternal source is unnecessary, since the forms of concepts and events are caused by the same causes that cause the concepts and events.

4. For detailed criticisms of naive realism, see my *Philosophy: An Introduction*, New York: Wiley, 1953, 38-49.   Reproduced in *Ethics as a Behavioral Science*, Springfield, Ill.: Charles C. Thomas, 1974.

5. Sociobiologists are beginning to contribute to fuller understanding of values. Some interpret values as "genetic traits."   See Edward O. Wilson, *Sociobiology*. Cambridge, Mass.: Harvard University Press, 1975.

Five OTHER VALUE SCIENCES

1. Marxists, accepting prevalent Western misconceptions, mistakenly believe that they have abandoned religion when adopting atheism.   They have produced another religion having its basis primarily in political economy rather than in axiology, ethics, or studies of the nature of religion itself.

2. See *Policy Sciences*, published quarterly since 1970.

Six THE SCIENCE OF VALUES

1. In a letter dated 2 September 1975.

2. In a letter dated 4 September 1975.

3. In a letter dated 22 September 1975.

4. Approved Minutes of the 187th Meeting of the National Science Board, NSB-77-96, pp. 187-10, National Science Foundation, Washington, 25 March 1977.

5. In a letter dated 8 April 1977.

6. In a letter dated 28 April 1977.

7. In a letter dated 18 November 1977.

8. In a letter dated 6 March 1980.

9. Quoted from H. Guyford Stever's letter dated 2 September 1975.

10. In a letter dated 13 March 1980.

11. "The new promising trend which is of such great importance in modern science is the recognition of the ultimate inconsistency of Scientific Positivism -- the failure of the Positivist to subject science itself to a scientific analysis." Robert J. Baum, "A Philosophical/Historical Perspective on Contemporary Concerns and Trends in the Area of Science and Values," in *Newsletter 9* of the Program on Public Conception of Science, October, 1974, p. 35.   Harvard University Jefferson Physical Laboratory, Cambridge, Mass.

WORKS CITED

Adorno, Theodor W., Gretel Adorno, Rolf Tiedmann, eds. *Aesthetic Theory*. London: Routledge & Kegan Paul, 1984.

Agassi, Joseph. *Science in Flux*. Dordrecht: Reidel, 1975.

Airaksinen, Timo. *From Subjective Welfare to Social Value: Axiology in Methodological and Philosophical Perspective*. Helsinki: Suomalainen Tiedeakatemia, 1979.

Alexander, Samuel. *Beauty and Other Forms of Value*. London: Macmillan, 1933.

Alport, Gordon. *Personality: A Psychological Interpretation*. New York: Holt, 1937.

Arnold, Magda B. *Feelings and Emotions*. New York: Academic Press, 1970.

Arrow, J. Kenneth. *Social Choice and Individual Values*, 2nd ed. New York: Wiley, 1963.

Attfield, Robin. *A Theory of Value and Obligation*. London: Croom Helm, 1987.

Bahm, Archie J. "'Aesthetic Experience and Moral Experience." *Journal of Philosophy* 55:20 (25 September 1958): 837-846.

____. "The Aesthetics of Organicism." *Journal of Aesthetics and Art Criticism* 26:4 (Summer 1968): 449-459.

____. *Bhagavad Gita: The Wisdom of Krishna*. Bombay: Somaiya, 1970.

____. "Comparative Aesthetics." *Journal of Aesthetics and Art Criticism* 24:1 (Fall 1965): 109-119.

____. *Comparative Philosophy: Western, Indian, and Chinese Philosophies Compared*. New Delhi: Vikas; Albuquerque: World Books, 1977a.

____. "Degrees and Scales." *I.T.A. Humanidades* (São Paulo, Brasil) 12 (1976): 67-73.

____. *Ethics as a Behavioral Science*. Springfield, Ill.: Charles C Thomas, 1974a.

____. *The Heart of Confucius*. Tokyo: Weatherhill, 1969.

____. "Interdisciplinology: The Science of Interdisciplinary Research." *Nature and System* 2 (1980): 29-35.

____. "Is a Universal Science of Aesthetics Possible?" *Journal of Aesthetics and Art Criticism* 31:1 (Fall 1972): 3-7.

____. *Metaphysics: An Introduction*. New York: Harper, 1974b.

____. "Obstacles to Treating Ethics as a Science." *Ethics as a Behavioral Science*, ch. 1. Springfield, Ill.: Thomas, 1974a.

____. *Philosophy: An Introduction*. New York: Wiley, 1953.

____. *Philosophy - 1968*. Albuquerque: University of Mew Mexico Annual Research Lecture, 13 May 1968.

____. *The Philosopher's World Model*. Westport, Conn.: Greenwood Press, 1979.

____. "Rightness Defined." *Philosophy and Phenomenological Research* 8:2 (December 1947): 266-268.

____. *The Specialist*. New Delhi: Macmillan of India; Albuquerque: World Books, 1977c.

_____. "Systems Theory: Hocus Pocus or Holistic Science?" *General Systems* 14 (1969): 175-177.

_____. *The World's Living Religions*. New York: Dell, 1964.

_____. *Why Be Moral?* Albuquerque: World Books, 1992.

Baram, Michael S. "Technology Assessment and Social Control." *Science* 180: 4085 (4 May 1973): 465-773.

Barnett, Lincoln. "J. Robert Oppenheimer." *Life* 27:15 (10 October, 1949):138.

Bascom, John. *Aesthetics: Or the Science of Beauty*. Boston: Crosby & Nichols, 1862.

Beardsley, Monroe C. *Aesthetics: Problems in the Philosophy of Criticism*. New York: Harcourt-Brace, 1958.

Berlyne, D. E. Ed. *Studies in the New Experimental Aesthetics*. Washington: Hemisphere Publishing Corporation, 1974.

Blaug, Mark. *The Cambridge Revolution, Success or Failure: A Critical Analysis of Cambridge Theories of Value and Distribution*. London: Institute of Economic Affairs, 1974.

Bosanquet, Bernard. *A History of Aesthetic*. New York: Macmillan, 1892.

Boulding, Kenneth E. "Some Contributions of Economics to the General Theory of Values." *Scientific Monthly* 69:1 (January 1949): 290-296.

Branscomb, Lewis H. "Science in the White House." *Science* 196 (20 May 1977): 850.

Brentano, Franz Clemens. *Psychologie vom Empirischen Standpunkte*, 2 vols. Leipzig: Duncker, 1874.

Bronowski, J. "The Educated Man in 1984." *Science* 123 (April 1956): 710-712.

Buermeyer, Laurence. *The Aestheitc Experience*. Merion, Pa.: Barnes Foundation, 1924.

Bunge, Mario. *Scientific Research, Vol. I, The Search for System*. New York: Springer-Verlag, 1967.

Caravale, Giovanni A. and Domencio A. Tosato. *Ricardo and the Theory of Value, Distribution, and Growth*. London: Routledge, 1980.

Caws, Peter. *Science and the Theory of Value*. New York: Random House, 1967.

_____. *The Philosophy of Science*. Princeton: Van Nostrand, 1965.

Chamberlain, Edward. *Towards a More General Theory of Value*. New York: Oxford University Press, 1957.

Churchman, C. West. *Prediction and Optimal Decision: The Philosophical Issues of a Science of Values*. Chicago: University of Chicago Press, 1961.

Cirillo, Leonard and Seymour Wapner. *Value Presuppositions in Human Development*. Hillsdale, N.J.: Lawrence Erlbaum Associates, 1981.

Cohen, Morris R. *Studies in Philosophy and Science*. New York: Holt, 1949.

Conant, James B. *On Understanding Science*. New Haven: Yale University Press, 1947.

Cooper, Frederic G. *Munsell Manual of Color*. Baltimore: Munsell Color Company, 1941.

Creegan, Robert F. "Recent Trends in the Psychology of Values." *Present-Day*

Psychology, ed. A. A. Roback. New York: Philosophical Library, 1955, pp. 949-960.

DeLaguna, Theodore *Introduction to the Science of Ethics*. New York: Macmillan, 1914.

Dewey, John. *Experience and Nature*. Lasalle, Ill.: Open Court, 1925.

____. *Logic: The Theory of Inquiry*. New York: Holt, 1938.

____. *Theory of Valuation*. Chicago: University of Chicago Press, 1939.

Dickie, George et al., eds. *Aesthetics: A Critical Anthology*. New York: Saint Martin's Press, 1989.

Dukes, William. "Psychological Studies of Values." *The Psychological Bulletin* 52 (1955): 24-50.

Eaton, Howard O. *The Austrian Philosophy of Value*. Norman, Okla.: University of Oklahoma Press, 1930.

Eaton, Marcia M. *Basic Issues in Aesthetics*. Belmont, Cal.: Wadsworth Publishing Company, 1988.

Eatwell, John and Murray Milgate, eds. *Keynes's Economics and Theory of Value and Distribution*. New York: Oxford University Press, 1983.

Ehrenfels, Christian von. *System der Werttheorie*, 2 vols. Leipzig: O. R. Reisland, 1897-1898.

Feibleman, James M. *Scientific Method*. The Hague: Nijhoff, 1971.

Findlay, J. N. *Axiological Ethics*. London: Macmillan, 1970.

Fisher, Irving. *Mathematical Investigations in the Theory of Value and Price*. Fairfield, N.J.: A. M. Kelley, 1892.

Frondizi, Risieri. *What Is Value? An Introduction to Axiology*. Englewood Cliffs, N.J.: Prentice-Hall, 1963.

Gordon, Kate. *Esthetics*. New York: Holt, 1909.

Gotshalk, D. W. *Patterns of Good and Evil*. LaSalle. Ill.: Open Court, 1963.

Hall, E. W. *What Is Value?* New York: Humanities Press, 1952.

Hammond, William A. *A Bibliography of Aesthetics and the Philosophy of Fine Arts from 1900 to 1932*. New York: Longmans, 1934.

Haney, Lewis H. *History of Economic Thought*. New York: Macmillan, 1911.

Hartman, Robert S. *The Structure of Value: Foundations of a Scientific Axiology*. Urbana, Ill.: University of Illinois Press, 1967.

Hartmann, Eduard von. *Grundriss der Axiologie*. Bad Sachsa im Harz: H. Haacke, 1908.

Hermerén, Göran. *The Nature of Aesthetic Qualities*. Melbourne, Fla.: Kreiger Publishing Company, 1988.

Hill, D. W. *Science: Its Effect on Industry, Politics, War, Education, Religion, and Leadership*. Brooklyn, N.Y.: Chemical Publishing Company, 1946.

Hilliard, A. L. *The Forms of Value: The Extension of a Hedonistic Axiology*. New

York: Columbia University Press, 1950.

Hook, Sidney, ed. *Human Values and Economic Policy*. New York: New York University Press, 1967.

Izard, Carroll. *Human Emotions*. New York, Plenum Press, 1977.

Jacobs, Philip and James J. Flink. "Values and Their Functioning in Decision-Making." *American Behavioral Scientist*. Supplementary Volume 5 (May 1962): 1-38.

Jevons, F. R. *Science Observed*. London: Allen and Unwin, 1893.

Kantor, J. R. *The Logic of Modern Science*. Bloomington, Ind.: Principia Press, 1953.

Kemper, Theodore D. *A Social Interactive Theory of Emotions*. New York: Wiley, 1978.

Kuhn, Thomas H. *The Structure of Scientific Revolutions*. Chicago: University of Chicago Press, 1962.

Langfeld, H. S. *The Aesthetic Attitude*. New York: Harcourt Brace, 1920.

Laszlo, Erwin and James B. Wilbur, eds. *Human Values and Natural Sciences*. New York: Gordon and Breach, 1970.

_____. *Value Theory in Philosophy and the Social Sciences*. New York: Gordon and Breach Science Publishers, 1973.

Lee, Sander H., ed. *Inquiries into Values*. Lewiston, N.Y.: Edwin Mellen Press, 1988.

Lee, Vernon. *The Beautiful: An Introduction to Psychological Analysis*. London: Cambridge University Press, 1913.

Lepley, Ray. *Verifiability of Value*. New York: Columbia University Press, 1944.

Lewis, Clarence I. *An Analysis of Knowledge and Valuation*. LaSalle, Ill.: Open Court, 1946.

Lichtenstein, Peter M. *An Introduction to Post-Keynsian and Marxian Theories of Value and Price*. Armonk, N. Y.: M. E. Sharpe, 1983.

Lowenberg, Jacob. "Preanalytic and Postanalytic Data." *Journal of Philosophy* 24:1 (6 January 1927).

Mahesward, D. P. ed. *Towards a Theory of Value: Focus on David Recardo*. Bhopal: Progress Publishers, 1978.

McDougall, William. *An Introduction to Social Psychology*, rev. ed. Boston: John Luce, 1921.

McGrath, Earl James. "Science and General Education." *The Scientific Monthly* 71:2 (August 1950).

Mees, C. E. K. *The Path of Science*. New York: Wiley, 1946.

Meinong, Alexius. *Psychologish-Ethische Untersuchungen zur Wert-Theorie*. Graz: Lettschner-Lubensky, 1894.

Meynell, Hugo A. *The Nature of Aesthetic Value*. Albany, N.Y.: S.U.N.Y. Press,

Meynell, Hugo A. *The Nature of Aesthetic Value*. Albany, N.Y.: S.U.N.Y. Press, 1986.

Mill, John Stuart. *A System of Logic, Ratiocinative and Inductive, being a connected view of the principles of evidence and methods of scientific investigation*. London: Longmans, 1843.

____. *Utilitarianism*. London: Longmans, 1863.

Morawsksi, Stefan. *Inquiries into the Fundamentals of Aesthetics*. Cambridge Mass.: M.I.T.Press, 1974.

Muller, H. J. "Values, Scientific Method, and Psychoanalysis." *Psychiatry* 127 (1958): 625-627.

Nahm, Milton C. *Aesthetic Experience and Its Presuppositions*. New York: Harper, 1946.

Niell, Robin. *A New Theory of Value: The Canadian Economics of H. A. Ennis*. Toronto: University of Toronto Press, 1972.

Northrop, F. S. C. *The Logic of the Sciences and the Humanities*. New York: Macmillan, 1947.

Osborne, Harold. *Aesthetics*. London: Oxford University Press, 1972.

Parker, DeWitt H. *Human Values*. New York: Harper, 1931.

____. *The Philosophy of Value*. Ann Arbor: University of Michigan Press, 1957.

____. *The Principles of Aesthetics*. Boston: Silver, Burdett, 1920.

Patanjali. *Yoga Sutras*, Part II, Sutra 9. Ed. Archie J. Bahm, *Yoga: Union With The Ultimate*. New York: Ungar, 1961.

Peirce, Charles Sanders. "The Fixation of Belief," *Popular Science Monthly* 13 (1877): 1-15.

Pepper, Stephen C. *The Source of Value*. Berkeley, Cal.: University of California Press, 1958.

Perry, Ralph Barton. *General Theory of Value*. New York: Longmans, 1926.

Polanyi, Michael. *Science, Faith, and Society*. Chicago: University of Chicago Press, 1946.

Popper, Karl R. *The Logic of Scientific Discovery*. London: Hutchinson, 1959.

Prall, D. W. *A Study in the Theory of Value*. Berkeley, Cal.: University of California Publications, 1921.

Puffer, Ethel. *The Psychology of Beauty*. Boston: Houghton Mifflin, 1905.

Rapport, Samuel B. and Helen Wright, eds. *Science: Method and Meaning*. New York: New York University Press, 1963.

Ravetz J. R. *Scientific Knowledge and Its Problems*. London: Oxford University Press, 1971.

Reid, John R. *A Theory of Value*. New York: Scribner's, 1938.

Rescher, Nicholas. *Introduction to Value Theory*. Englewood Cliffs, N.J.: Prentice-Hall, 1969.

Ritchie, A. D., *Scientific Method*. London: Routedge, 1923.

Robbins, Lionel. *An Essay on the Nature and Significance of Economic Science*. London: Macmillan, 1932.

Ross, Stephen David. *The Scientific Process*. The Hague: Nijhoff, 1971.

Ross, W. D. ed. *The Works of Aristotle Translated into English*, v. 9. *Ethica Nicomachea* by W. D. Ross. *Magna Moralia* by St. George Stock. *Ethica Eudemia* by J. Solomon. Oxford: Clarendon Press, 1925.

Santayana, George. *The Sense of Beauty*. New York: Scribner's, 1896.

Schorr, J. E. "The Development of a Test to Measure the Intensity of Values." *Journal of Educational Psychology* 44 (1953): 266-274.

Science 182a (1973): 9-178.

Sewall, Hannah Robie. *The Theory of Value Before Adam Smith*. New York: A. M. Kelley, 1901.

Singer, Charles. *A Short History of Scientific Ideas*. London: Oxford University Press, 1959.

Snow, C.P. "The Moral Neutrality of Science." *The New Scientist*. Eds. Paul C. Ober and Herman A. Estrin. Garden City, N.Y.: Doubleday, 1962.

Sperry, R. W. "Mind, Brain, and Human Values." *Bulletin of the Atomic Scientists* 22:7 (September 1966): 3.

____. "Science and the Problem of Human Values." *Perspectives in Biology and Medicine* 16:1 (Autumn 1972): 115-130.

____. "Science and the Problem of Human Values." *Zygon: The Journal of Religion and Science* 9:1 (March 1974): 18.

Strong, Tracy B. *Aesthetics and the Search for Political Authority*. Boulder, Colo.: Westview Press, 1993.

Taylor, F. Sherwood. *Concerning Science*. London: Macdonald, 1949.

Temmer, Mark. *Time in Rousseau and Kant*. Geneva: Droz, 1958.

Thompson, J. Arthur. *An Introduction to Science*. New York: Holt, 1911.

Thompson, Jack George. *The Psychology of Emotions*. New York: Plenum Press, 1988.

Thurstone, L. L. "The Measurement of Values." *Psychological Review* 61 (1954): 47-58.

Turner, Frederick. *Beauty: The Value of Values*. Charlottesville, Va.: University Press of Virginia, 1992.

Urban, Wilbur Marshall. *Valuation: Its Nature and Laws*. London: Sonnenschein, 1909.

Weisz, Paul B. *Elements of Biology*. New York: McGraw-Hill, 1961.

Werkmeister, W. H. *Historical Spectrum of Value Theories*. Lincoln, Neb.: Johnson Publishing Co., 1973.

White, Ralph K. *Value Analysis: The Nature and Use of Its Methods*. Glen Gardner, N.J.: Society for the Psychological Study of Social Issues, 1951.

Whitehead, Alfred North and Bertrand Russell. *Principia Mathematica*, 3 vols. Cambridge, England: Cambridge University Press, 1910-1913.

Wilk, Stan. *Humanistic Anthropology*. Knoxville: University of Tennessee Press, 1991.

Wilson, Edward O. Quoted by Nicholas Wade, "Sociobiology: Troubled Birth for New Discipline." *Science* 191 (10 March 1976): 1153.

Young, Jeffrey T. *Classical Theories of Value: From Smith to Sraffa*. Boulder, Colo.: Westview Press, 1978.

INDEX OF PERSONS

Adorno, Theodor W., 107, 123
Agassi, Joseph, 31, 123
Alexander, Samuel, 107, 123
Alport, Gordon, 20, 122
Aquinas, 104
Aristotle, 103, 108
Arnold, Amagda B., 112, 123
Arrow, Kenneth J., 110, 123
Attfield, Robin, 105, 123

Baram, Michael S., 34, 124
Barnett, Lincoln, 33, 124
Bascom, John, 106, 124
Baum, Robert J., 115, 121
Beardsley, Monroe C., 107, 124
Benedict, Ruth, 113
Bentham, Jeremy, 104
Berlyne, D.E., 107, 124
Blaug, Mark, 110, 124
Bosanquet, Bernard, 107, 124
Boulding, Kenneth E., 110, 124
Branscomb, L.B., 101, 124
Brentano, Franz, 104, 124
Bronowski, J., 35, 124
Buermeyer, Laurance, 107, 124
Bunge, Mario, 26, 124

Calvin, 104
Caravale, Giovanni A., 110, 124
Caws, Peter, 19, 105, 124
Chamberlain, Edward, 110, 124
Churchman, C.West, 105, 124
Cirillo, Leonard, 112, 124
Cohen, Morris R., 19, 124
Conant, James B., 33, 124
Cooper, Fredric G., 87, 124
Creegan, Robert F., 111, 125

DeLaguna, Theodore, 108, 125
Dewey, John, 23, 32, 105, 125
Dickie, George, 107, 125
Dukes, William, 111, 125

Eaton, Howard O., 104, 125
Eaton, Marcia M., 107, 125
Eatwell, John, 110, 125
Ehrenfels, Christian von, 104, 125

Feibleman, James K., 19, 29, 125
Findlay, J.N., 105, 125
Fisher, Irving, 109, 110, 125
Flink, James J., 101, 126
Frondizi, Risieri, 105, 125

Gordon, Kate, 107, 125
Gotshalk, D.W., 105, 125

Hackerman, Norman, 116
Hall, E.W., 105, 125
Hammond, William A., 107, 125
Haney, Lewis H., 109, 125
Hartman, Robert S., 105, 125
Hartmann, Eduard von, 104, 107, 125
Hermerén, Göran, 108, 125
Hill, D.W., 33, 125
Hilliard, A.L., 105, 125
Hook, Sidney, 110, 126

Izard, Carrol, 111, 112, 126

Jacobs, Philip, 101, 126
Jevons, F.R., 19, 23, 33, 126

Kantor, J.R., 29, 126
Kemper, Theodore D., 112, 126
Kuhn, Thomas H., 18, 20, 30, 126

INDEX OF SUBJECTS

actual values, 57-62
aesthetics, 94-96, 106-108
American Pragmatism, 21
Anandism, 42, 46-47, 51, 52
anthropology, 113
apparent values, 64-66
appearance, 73
applied science, 32-34
art, 95-97
axiology, 3-9, 103-106, 114

bad, 37-39
beauty, 94-95
biology, 110
British Empiricist 2-22

complex inferences, 85-86
conceptual inference, 79-83
crises, 6-9
curiosity, 12-13

data, 73-74
deductive inference, 84-85

economics, 100, 109
ends, 40-57
epistemology, 3-4, 72-91
ethics, 97, 108-109, 114
evaluative judgments, 69
Existentialism, 120

good, 37-39, 52, 114

Hedonism, 42-43, 49, 52
hedonistic paradox, 43

inductive inference, 83-84
inference, 78-86, 88-91
instrumental values, 40-41, 62-63, 66,
    69, 87-88, 91
intrinsic values, 41-57, 62-63, 65-66, 69,
    86-87, 88-91
intuition, 72-78, 86-88, 120

Logical Realists, 119

Marxists, 121
means, 40-57
metaphysics, 3-4
method, 18-28
mixed values, 67

Naive Realism, 80

objective values, 62-64
objectivity, 3-17

perceptual inference, 78-79
policy sciences, 101
potential values, 57-62
Pragmatic Realism, 21-22, 81-83, 90-91
presuppositions, 26-28
problems, 11-12
psychology, 111-112
pure values, 67

real values, 64-66
religiology, 97-99, 109
Romanticism, 44-46, 50-51, 52

VALUE INQUIRY BOOK SERIES

VIBS

1. Noel Balzer, **The Human Being as a Logical Thinker.**

2. Archie J. Bahm, **Axiology: Science of Values.**

3. H. P. P. (Hennie) Lötter, **Justice for an Unjust Society.**